THE EXPRESS YEARS

Jack Webster was born in 1931 in the village of Maud, Aberdeenshire. As a child he suffered from a serious heart condition and there was no certainty that he would ever be able to work. But his determination to fulfil a boyhood dream of becoming a journalist overcame this problem and at the age of sixteen he started work on the *Turriff Advertiser*. He later moved on to the *Evening Express* and *The Press and Journal* in Aberdeen, before joining the *Scottish Daily Express* in Glasgow. After a highly successful period as a features writer with the *Express*, he is now a popular columnist with *The Herald*. Jack Webster lives in Glasgow.

Also by Jack Webster:

The Dons (1978)
A Grain of Truth (1981)
Gordon Strachan (1984)
Another Grain of Truth (1988)
'Tis Better to Travel (1989)
Alistair MacLean: A Life (1991)
Famous Ships of the Clyde (1993)
Grains of Truth (1994)

Films (television and video):

Webster's Roup (1985)
As Time Goes By (1987)
Northern Lights (1989)
Webster Goes West (1991)
The Glory of Gothenburg (1993)
John Brown: The Man Who Drew a Legend (1994)

THE EXPRESS YEARS

A GOLDEN DECADE

JACK WEBSTER

EDINBURGH
B&W PUBLISHING
1994

First published 1994
by B&W Publishing, Edinburgh
© Express Newspapers plc
ISBN 1 873631 36 7

British Library Cataloguing in Publication Data:
A catalogue record for this book is available
from the British Library

PRINTED BY WERNER SÖDERSTRÖM

CONTENTS

ACKNOWLEDGEMENTS

Special thanks to Express Newspapers plc for their
kind permission to use these articles which first
appeared in the *Scottish Daily Express*.

Thanks also to *The Herald* for permission to use
the photographs in this edition, except for
the photograph of Field-Marshal Montgomery
which is by kind permission
of Camera Press Ltd, London.

THE SWINGING SIXTIES

The closing decade of the century has led me rather neatly to the final decade of my own career in daily journalism. And in terms of personal satisfaction, what a career it has turned out to be. From the bleak outlook of a boy with heart trouble, leaving school at fourteen sickly and depressed, I somehow gained the favour of the gods in a way which leaves a doubt that I may yet awake from a dream.

The joy does not abate even in the autumn of my career, in which I enjoy something of a following for a personal column which appears in *The Herald* every Tuesday. In the civilised atmosphere of *The Herald* in Albion Street, Glasgow, there is time to craft the regular 900 words, a vehicle for distilling the thoughts and experiences of half a century and hanging them on some topical peg.

One day, though not quite yet, I would like to bring the best of those columns into book form. For the moment, however, I have chosen to revisit an earlier phase of my journalism when life was more frenetic, when youthful exuberance was taking me here, there and everywhere, in that period loosely labelled as the Swinging Sixties.

Having started as a lad on the *Turriff Advertiser* in the aftermath of the Second World War and spent the entire decade of the fifties on the Aberdeen *Press and Journal* and *Evening Express*, I left my native North-east for the wider world of journalism at the beginning of 1960. It was Leap Year Night, in fact, when I stepped inside this same Albion Street building which was then the home of the *Scottish Daily Express*, the favoured child of the founding Lord Beaverbrook, who was bred from a Scots Presbyterian minister and brought up in Canada before he settled in London and turned his

Daily Express into the most widely-read newspaper in the world.

But he did not rest until there was a Scottish end to that empire and, in 1928, he took over an old tobacco factory in the heart of Glasgow and was on his way to giving the land of his fathers its biggest-selling daily paper.

In those more expansive days I was joining a throbbing hive of journalism, where Beaverbrook employed 2000 people. My own quiet role was that of a sub-editor; but there is a limited appeal in refining other people's work and it dawned on me that, if I had the capability to improve upon the writing of the writer, I would be better doing the damned thing myself! What's more, instead of spending my life at a desk, working till 2am, I could be out and about absorbing the rhythms of an exciting world. In the twelve years before reaching the *Express*, I had become well grounded in reporting. But how could I break into feature writing? There was only one answer: WRITE. So from time to time I placed an article under the nose of Drew Rennie, the ebullient Dundonian in charge of features. He liked the way I wrote and published it.

Drew Rennie was a tough cookie with a soft centre, as I discovered one day when he paced up and down the office before plucking up courage to ask a question which embarrassed him. In the news schedule that day was a story about a British soldier being court-martialled for desertion. His defence was that he had a bad stammer and couldn't stand the tormenting of his mates any longer; so he ran away. I too had been plagued by a stammer all my life, an impediment which troubled me greatly as a reporter. Drew Rennie wanted to know if I could bring myself to write an article explaining the plight of the deserting soldier. Of course I could. As relief broke over his face, however, I took the chance to remind him that I would like to do this on a permanent basis.

Coincidentally, *Express* editor Ian MacColl had evidently decided I should now be making a choice between sub-editing and writing. It was an easy choice and that was how I became a feature writer in the very early days of what came to be known as the Swinging Sixties.

Actually, that pulsating period did not oblige by arriving so precisely as 1960. I would place its origins around 1963, that year of titillation and tragedy which began by rocking the Tory Party with the Profumo Scandal and ended by rocking the whole of mankind with the assassination of President Kennedy. These bizarre events seemed to stir a potent cocktail of human emotion, bursting the dams of self-control with devilish force and creating a sense of liberation, real or otherwise. Sex ran riot and at a heady time of much employment and economic prosperity, set to the rhythms of Beatlemania, there eventually came a notion that we were engaged in a carefree Swinging Sixties. The phrase itself, as I remember it, came late and the mood which prompted it was already spilling over towards the 1970s.

Well, that is how I observed it anyway. I reckon it was petering out around 1973 so, for the purposes of this book, I have gathered a selection of what I was doing as a feature writer in that high-charged period. I don't know if it brings any flavour of the Swinging Sixties but it should give some hint of the topics which reached the breakfast table.

Unearthing these old articles has enabled me to gauge my development as a journalist. Mostly they were written on the day, often conceived in the forenoon for delivery by teatime. That was how the *Express* worked. Sometimes the haste shows through; at other times I am pleasantly surprised by a phrase cooked up in the urgency of the moment which might not occur to me now. I have left the articles as they were written, with whatever spontaneity or imperfection.

I merely look back on that period as a golden decade of my *Express* years, with the affection of one who remembers the joy of learning his craft. So join me now on a nostalgic ramble through my thirties, a reminder of what I was doing in journalism, day by day a generation ago. . . .

*for Ian MacColl and Drew Rennie
—highly professional journalists
who gave me the opportunity*

ON A SATURDAY MORNING
22 YEARS AGO

2nd September 1961

In the grey, wet misery of that September Saturday, we waited in our small village, waited for an event that seemed, to the child mind, bigger than the impending war itself.

For this was something we could understand, the arrival of a train-load of youngsters like ourselves, Glasgow boys and girls coming to live in our village, as our guests, far from the bombs that were bound to come to Clydeside.

Earlier in the day the local "Terriers" had streamed out, away, they said, to France to fight.

But that was far away. Life was here in the heart of Aberdeenshire, as we watched the train appear from the mists and wheeze its way to a stop at the station platform.

Out they tumbled, all 200 of them, to be marched in a pathetic file to the village hall, where they were allocated to our homes.

We looked at each other sheepishly and the Glaswegian, as so often, was the first to break the ice.

"How are ye, Mac?" We didn't know anyone called Mac but said we were fine and soon we were friends, a strange alliance of city slicker and country clumsy.

They had seen the "flicks", which were a rarity in our

1

experience. But we had seen a cow calving and we knew that a bull wasn't born with a ring in its nose, which put us at least on level terms.

They had ships and chips and pubs and parks. But we had woods and fields and tractors. Ach, that was nothing to compare with ships and chips, etc. Oh, yes, it was. Oh, no, it wasn't . . .

So they became Glesca Keelies and we became country unprintables.

Meanwhile Hitler was rumbling on, all but unnoticed on the horizon of our childish world.

We played, we quarrelled, we went to school together, each lending something to the culture of the other.

But the draw of the city became too much for most of the Glasgow evacuees.

Gradually they drifted back, away to the back streets and the bombs, to the sight of their ships and the smell of their chips.

Some we were glad to see go; to others we extended a manly hand of "Let's shake despite our differences".

For some, there were actually tears, the heartbreak of friendships made, now to be broken. In our small village we returned to the peace we had known, but life, I'm glad to say, was never quite the same.

We had learned from them. And they undoubtedly had learned from us.

On this Saturday morning, exactly 22 years after those Glasgow urchins descended on us—and on scores of other village communities up and down the country—I am thinking of them now.

Perhaps the fresh rumblings from Berlin point the memory. I wonder where they are, the Hammy Steels, the Myer Singers, the Mary Lindsays.

Perhaps they, too, have their memories this Saturday

morning. To them—whose children must now be nearing the age that we were then—I say: "Haste ye back. For you are sure of a very special welcome."

IT'S BLACKPOOL ON A
BLEAK SCOTTISH BRAE AS
OLD AIKEY'S FAIR LIVES ON...

21st July 1962

Chair-o-planes spinning, buskers bawling, music blaring and the preachers admonishing the milling thousands about this devilish desecration of the Sabbath.

It will all happen tomorrow, not in some Continental playground or even in Blackpool, but on a lonely Scottish hillside, within a few hundred yards of the historic Abbey of Deer, in Aberdeenshire.

It is Aikey Fair—the day when 30,000 couthy country folk cast off the popular image of themselves and enter into a festival of abandon that may surprise the outside world.

They come by bus, or bicycle—even on foot—to frolic around a fairground that attracts a varied assortment of gipsies and cheapjacks, salesmen and pickpockets.

Dour, sensible folk, who wrest a living from the land, will wear a "Kiss-me-quick" hat, slobber over candy floss, flock into the Wall of Death, the boxing booth or, if there is no kent face about, sidle into the variety booth, where some shapely lady is liable to wear nothing but a smile.

How did it all start? Some will tell you that the people of Aberdeenshire were gathering at the same spot—between the villages of Maud and Old Deer—800 years ago. But

4

popular legend has it that, on a certain Wednesday in the mid 17th century, a wandering packman named Aikey was crossing the nearby River Ugie on stepping stones when he stumbled and fell into the water.

He laid out his wares to dry and people passing stopped to buy his gay collection. Delighted with his lucrative tumble and being perhaps the forefather of the high-powered salesman, old Aikey announced that he would be back next year on the same day. He kept his date and, without the preliminary of a dooking, spread out his wares for another day's brisk business.

More people came to sell and more to buy and Aikey Fair became the annual gathering of farming folk, the biggest horse market for miles around.

Hundreds of animals would tread the country roads to Aikey on that July Wednesday to be bought and sold by farmers and dealers from all over the country. Accounts were settled, drams were downed and many a shelt instinctively drove its gig and comatose master home to the croft at the end of the day.

The Sunday revelry did not begin until 1926. Show people always gathered a few days before the Wednesday Fair, and for several years crowds had come to watch on the preceding Sunday. In that year, one astute showman—maybe a descendant of old Aikey?—started his merry-go-round.

The crowds stood abashed, gave it a second thought, threw caution to the wind and Aikey Sunday was here to stay. The Wednesday market survived but, as the horse population declined, the emphasis changed to the Sunday.

In 1939, Benny Lynch was there, sparring 48 rounds with Freddy Tennant, and saying: "I'll be back, and if I get to the top again, I'll stay there."

The war was upon us and Benny never came back. But

Aikey did.

But by 1951 there were only 60 horses for sale on the Wednesday and next year came the end of Aikey Wednesday. There were only six people—and one piebald pony for sale.

But the Sunday goes on and on and on. The smell of fish and chips and toffee apples mingles with the scent of the heather on the hill. The cacophony of the fairground echoes in the shell of the old abbey down the brae.

Perhaps the echo is more than just a noise. Perhaps it is the echo of generations past, a continuing link with fore-fathers who have sweated on the grudging lands of Buchan but who sought this annual day of relief.

Some may see Aikey as nothing but a pagan rabble. But might there not be a touch of religion as well?

MONTGOMERY AND ME

It was really curiosity about the political scene which took me to Yugoslavia. But politics were soon forgotten as I sampled the delights of the Dalmatian coast and discovered that the most unexpected things can happen there.

Here in Dubrovnik was warmth and relaxation as we dream about them and there I lay, soaking in the sun and viewing the villas nearby, whose terraced gardens swept down to the shores.

"Who could live in such luxury in this land of equality?" I asked myself. A local resident soon put me right.

"That one there, for example, is a guest house for Tito's V.I.P.'s," he said. "The great war man Montgomery is there now."

That evening I had gained myself an invitation to be Monty's guest and there we sat in the warm evening air, engaged in conversation that was sometimes jovial and then serious.

This was a novel experience in more ways than one. As a journalist, it was the first time I had ever *been* interviewed. I had seen things which were not included in the field-marshal's official tour.

7

What was the agriculture like? How were the people in their homes?

In the midst of the questions Monty, who is not a drinker, granted me a vermouth. And he called a gentleman to fetch it.

When the drink was served I dismissed the waiter perfunctorily. I took one gulp, one second look at the "waiter"— and realised that he was none other than Popovic, the Foreign Secretary.

We talked about Alamein and the glories of Monty's life . . . and about "last weekend when I was visiting Winston". I listened with fascination to the more intimate side of great men's lives.

When it was time to leave the fairyland world of Villa Scheherazade, its lights glistening from the trees on the waterfalls below, Monty bade me pass on his regards to my chief, his old friend Lord Kemsley.

I wondered if this was just a gesture, since he knew that I was not likely to be in contact with my superior.

But I took no chances and conveyed his message. A few days later, Kemsley received a letter: "I hope your man Webster told you that . . . Signed Montgomery of Alamein."

As I say, the most unexpected things can happen in Dubrovnik.

THE LEGEND OF GAVIN GREIG
COMES ALIVE

August 1964

All my days I have lived with a legend. The legend of Gavin Greig—poet, playwright, composer, closely related to Edvard Grieg, and even more closely related to me. He was my great-grandfather.

His novels line the family bookshelves, his plays are still performed all over the country—50 years after his death—and folk singers from America come on pilgrimages to a little corner of Aberdeenshire to honour the man who saved so many of Scotland's folk songs from extinction.

I knew the legend. But recently I had one of those rare encounters with history. Into my office came a well-preserved gentleman who said he had a clear picture of the man in person.

Alec Cruickshank, complete with luggit bonnet, is 97. He lives in Prestwick but his roots are in Turriff, Aberdeenshire, where he learned to be a blacksmith around 1882.

Alec played the fiddle and conducted the local orchestra. That was how he came to meet Gavin Greig.

"His play *Mains's Wooin'* was all the talk at the end of last century. So we decided to stage it at Turriff. My brother George and I hired a landau and went to the Schoolhouse of Whitehill, Aberdeenshire, where Gavin Greig was dominie," said Alec. "And there we met the man we had heard so much about. He was a tall, lean man, gaunt and with a slight stoop. You wouldn't have called him good looking but he was a scholarly man, a brilliant conversationalist and full of humour.

"When we put on the play, the following spring, he came by horse bus to see it and I gave him a bed for the night. The streets were deserted every night that week, for everybody was there to see *Mains's Wooin'*."

Gavin Greig, the humble woodcutter's son from Dyce, went on to write other Scottish classics, novels such as *Logie O' Buchan* and plays like *Prince Charlie*. *Mains's Wooin'* had its most lavish production only last year and is still being produced by amateur companies, even in England.

With a twinkle in his old eyes, Alec Cruickshank twirled his moustache, bade me a cheery goodbye and went home.

And here I sit, thinking about my famous forefather. If the strings of heredity are pulling at me now it is perhaps a reminder that, without him, I might not have felt the desire to write this.

SO MANY NAMES
FOR ONE BABY!

29th August 1964

It was such a problem. And suddenly it was an even bigger problem. The difficulty of finding a name for the new-born babe became the difficulty of knowing what *not* to call him as *Express* readers poured out their imaginations in response to my plea.

The choice ranged through Stephen (excellent), Lawrence (adventurous), Brian (middle class), Vincent (classy) to Conrad, Derek, Winston and Stuart.

One gentleman was desperate for Dan. It sounded such a fine name and there had been so many famous Dans like Dan McGrew and "Dan . . . Dan" you know the rest). There was prejudice, of course. The writer was Dan Reid, of Florence Drive, Giffnock.

Stuart Paul, of Arundel Drive, Glasgow, was a Shakespeare man to the ruffles. Laertes or Claudius or Hamlet were his suggestions, but I could foresee difficulties. Mr Paul, however, was not an unreasonable man. He had a reserve, the classical name for a boy—Lycidas, from Greek mythology.

While the poets were scrabbling in obscurity at the Festival, the versifiers were rushing to my rescue. One lady from

11

Abernethy wrote:

> *Hullo, little lonely stranger;*
> *Are you looking for a name;*
> *What about D'Arcy Dagenham,*
> *If you want to rise to fame?*
> *You could still be useful and happy—*
> *And it wouldn't matter a damn,*
> *If your name were Billy or Bobby,*
> *Or Jeremiah or Tam.*

Easily the most popular choice was David (meek and mild and beloved). But someone touched on Keith and that set my wife and me thinking afresh.

After all, her own maiden name was Keith. She is descended from the family of that famous Scottish soldier, the Earl Marischal. And we have other skeletons in the cupboard.

Our nameless one is also descended from the families of Sir Henry Raeburn, the painter, Edvard Grieg, national composer of Norway, and, perhaps closest of all, from our own National Bard.

My own middle name is Barron and "Barron Webster" has an author's ring about it. So we spent an evening on permutations and yesterday, only minutes before I was due to become liable for prosecution at the hands of the registrar, I dashed along to the office.

What did we finally call the baby?

KEITH BARRON RAEBURN WEBSTER

And he will probably think we're nuts.

A DOG'S LIFE—BUT IT
MADE MY WORLD
A BRIGHTER PLACE

One fine August day when I was a boy, with the sun hot in the sky and the corn rustling in the wind, my father arrived home with an unwanted dog, a poor cowering waif he had saved from being shot.

The dog was uncertain of his welcome but as he crept nervously away to a corner we accepted the fact that there was now an extra member of the family.

Through ill-use and the narrow escape from the firing squad, he had acquired poor opinions of the human race, treating every two-legged animal with suspicion. So we set about feeding him back to health, restoring his confidence and showing him the kinder side of life.

Nigger was a cross between a Black Labrador and a Collie, the cross that produces some of the rarest qualities in a dog. And if he needed a passport to the heart it was in those large, strangely frank, brown eyes.

By Christmas of that year his world was a better place to live in. He was well on the way to believing once more in the possibilities of humanity.

That Christmas morning Nigger acted with uncanny timing by disappearing at an unlikely moment and arriving back with a live chick, held gently in his mouth. He set the chick at my mother's feet. It was festive gratitude to the folk who had saved his life. But the chicken had been stolen from a neighbour and had to be returned.

The gentle mouth that could bear the delicacy of a live chick could just as easily turn vicious when the occasion demanded.

Nigger became known as the finest rat-dog in the district, treating every rodent creature with contempt.

More and more he acquired the finer attitudes of the human being, with none of the flaws. More and more he came to make us glad that my father had arrived just before the trigger was pulled.

For 16 years—an uncommonly long time for a big dog— Nigger shared our home, heightened our joys, lessened our sorrows and taught humanity to the humans.

Where else can you depend on such loyalty and gratitude and understanding? Where else can you find such solid worth that is not swayed by the pendulum of fashion and frailty?

These were the things I was thankful for yesterday, as always. The sun was shining and the corn was still rustling in the breeze.

But it was not so bright an August day. At least one cloud hung heavy in the sky. For yesterday my Nigger died.

A BOY BETRAYED—BY THE LANGUAGE OF LOVE

———————— *September 1964* ————————

On the gentle slopes of Aberdeenshire, where I grew up, a man was a man and he proved it by exaggerating all the outward signs of manliness.

"The wife" was an inferior creature, fine for keeping the house, carrying the coal, producing the children and other chores like that.

Her status was at least equal to that of a good sheepdog or a willing Clydesdale.

And for that she was supposed to be thankful. It used to surprise me that children appeared at all, for the one word that men-folk hardly mentioned was "love".

It was a soft, uncomfortable word, embodying tenderness and if there is one thing my rural kinsmen can't stand it is the suggestion of tenderness. To them it has a ring of balminess.

So I grew up with the impression that love was a necessary evil, to be brushed under the carpet or behind the haystack— a subject for the bawdy crack or the sly experiment but never to be talked of openly or seriously.

Follow my footsteps, then, on the night I first plucked up courage to ask home with a girl from a dance.

There I was, a long strip of 15-year-old, trailing her up the road as if she didn't belong to me and I had just been asked to tow her home.

She might have been a broken-down car or a breeding sow. Only I would have looked a bit stupid if I had had thoughts of kissing a breeding sow. And thoughts I had.

For she was an attractive girl, a little older and a little more experienced than I.

Once I had run through the price of corn and the condition of the turnips and made a fleeting reference to the moon, I launched into the question which I had been composing and rehearsing for days.

"Do you mind," I said, "if I kiss you?"

There was a moment of silence, then she replied with emphasis: "No!"

Before I tell you what happened, please read these last two sentences again and see what interpretation you would put on her meaning.

My reaction was to bolt. Like a runaway horse I louped a dyke and ran till I reached the safety of my own home.

I lay panting on top of my bed, cursing the ingratitude of women and vowing what I would do to that muckle moon, still smirking his way across the sky.

It was not till later that she explained sweetly that her "No!" was not a rejection but an invitation. She was an intelligent girl and had simply answered my question. No, she did not mind.

To emphasise the point she presented me with a copy of Dickens' *Great Expectations*. I presented myself with a copy of the *New English Grammar*.

Indeed, soon afterwards she had cause to write to me of her "unrequited love". Not being familiar with "unrequited" I thought she has mis-spelled "unrequired" and hastily wrote back to assure her that she was greatly mistaken.

After the frustration of our moonlight misunderstanding her love was badly required! So we settled to a beautiful romance which blossomed and faded. And here I am, committing the unpardonable sin of telling you about it.

Even today, nearly 20 years later, I am haunted by the spectacle of that very first night of love.

Haunted by the thought of a warm-hearted young lady closing her dreamy eyes, poising her eager lips and drawing the quiver of her body towards the shadow of an idiot already disappearing over a six-foot dyke in the distance.

I am not here to theorise upon the effect of early experience, but it is a fact that the lady has remained to this day a spinster.

Such are the hazards and the ironies of life. And such is the material of memories.

AS GUID SCOTS TONGUES
STOP WAGGIN'

————————— *2nd October 1964* —————————

With a faintly sad expression, the man in the big chair gazed out on the autumn calm of Edinburgh's George Square and supplied the answer to my query: Just how much spoken Scots is still in daily use today?

"It varies from Glasgow, where it is pretty well dead already, to Aberdeenshire, where around 50 per cent of the people still speak their native tongue regularly," he says.

David Murison is the brilliant Scot who has given over his life to the mammoth task of preserving our native language.

As editor of the Scottish National Dictionary, he published one more volume this week, reaching the word "naither," which, of course, is "neither."

"I sometimes wonder if the dictionary or myself will reach Z first," he says with a smile. But with any luck he should be finished in about nine years.

Then Scotland will have a heritage of words preserved in detail for those who care. But who does?

"Oddly enough, it is the Americans, the Russians, Japanese, Swedes and Dutch who are showing a great interest in our culture and therefore in our language," he says. "It is a disgrace that it has to be left to other people."

David Murison is a couthy lad of pairts. At 51 he shows more signs of his solid Fraserburgh background than his scholarly years at Cambridge.

If he were a man capable of bitterness he would lay much of the blame for the dilution of the native tongue at the door of schools.

"Ay, there is snobbery involved here," he will tell you. "It is counted a social handicap that militates against advancement if you speak Scots.

"Why, you only have to listen to 'Top of the Form' to find that the questions which most stump Scots children are the Scottish ones."

Mr Murison turned his gaze out to George Square again, where Walter Scott spent his early years.

"In this very square, the gentry of Edinburgh were speaking Scots in the eighteenth century. Then the judges and advocates began imitating the English; the Select Society was formed to acquire standard English, and Scots speech moved to the middle classes. The rot had set in."

In the face of much indifference, David Murison and his four graduate assistants forge ahead with their task of dedication. It was first mooted in 1907, carried on by Dr William Grant, of Aberdeen, and finally taken over by Mr Murison in 1946. "In 100 years from now, Scots words may not be used at all," he confesses.

"The intonations will last for a long time—the vowel sounds and so on. Of course, I am a born pessimist. That way I only get pleasant surprises. But I must admit that at times I see a glimmer of hope for our language. It may yet come back into use—as a fashion."

David Murison talked to me for two hours, mostly in the broadest of Scots. Its music was with me as I walked out into the historic air of George Square.

19

Then I spotted a bulldozer and pondered an ominous fact
. . . these fine old buildings are due for demolition.

PS: Thirty years after this article, David Murison was living in retirement in Fraserburgh.

IS THIS THE TRUTH ABOUT
BONNIE PRINCE CHARLIE?

———————— *9th December 1964* ————————

Do you still think of Bonnie Prince Charlie with a gentle ache in your heart, with dew in your eye, and the muted strains of "Over the Sea to Skye" humming in your head? Do you harbour an image of the great Scottish hero who ran into a bit of bad luck at a place called Culloden?

If so, prepare yourself for a shock from two men I spoke to yesterday. BBC producer Peter Watkins and author John Prebble. Next Tuesday, Mr Watkins will present a 75-minute television documentary programme which seeks to reconstruct the Culloden catastrophe, sweeping away much of the romance and replacing it with more factual matter.

Mr Watkins takes a most unromantic view of Charles. "He was a stupid, impulsive, vain and selfish young man," he told me at BBC Television Centre yesterday.

"He was not particularly good-looking, and he didn't have a clear-cut mind, and when the time came he left the sinking ship and never thought very much about the Highlander again."

Mr Watkins (29) came to Scotland to film his documentary and used ordinary people instead of actors. He could not set his scene in Culloden which is now under forest, but

21

he found a suitable spot near Loch Ness.

John Prebble comes into the picture because it was after reading his book on Culloden that Mr Watkins set out on five months of research into the whole gory business.

Mr Prebble has been historical adviser to the programme.

But Mr Prebble, like Mr Watkins, is an Englishman. What is his special interest in this slice of Scottish history which is best remembered by many for the butchery of the English leader, Cumberland?

"I lived in Canada as a boy, in a town of Scots exiles, who awakened my interest in Scotland and soon I was fascinated by the history of the country.

"I have visited Scotland many times and now my elder son has married a Shetland girl and lives there."

Mr Prebble, who lives in Surrey, is at present writing a factual account of Glencoe.

About Culloden he says: "The tragedy of the '45 is not the tragedy of Prince Charles. It is the tragedy of the Highland people. They were fighting not so much for the Stuarts but for a way of life. The '45 was really the beginning of the end of the Highland way of life."

Mr Prebble believes that Prince Charlie did a great deal of harm to Scotland. But what about Cumberland?

"He was a professional soldier, but not a very good one, for Culloden was the only battle he ever won. As far as he was concerned, the clans were savages and rebels and as such were entitled to destruction," said Mr Prebble.

This, however, is not an attempt to whitewash Cumberland. The sympathies of these two men lie clearly with the Highlander for the raw deal he had at the hands of the Prince.

They are searching behind the romantic legend to tell us what is really supposed to have happened at Culloden.

But with Englishmen creeping upon us next Tuesday

evening, I expect more than a few Scots will be keeping a canny watch.

WHEN HAPPINESS MEANS
GIVING MONEY AWAY

——————————— *2nd December 1964* ———————————

The courteous gentleman in the fawn dressing-gown exercised his limbs with the delight of a child and told me of two burdens which he has at last managed to shed.

The first is rheumatoid arthritis, which he has conquered after two years in bed. The second is a small matter of £2 million, which he has finally managed to spread around in the cause of human happiness.

Charles Hepburn, the 73-year-old Glasgow whisky magnate, sighed with unmistakable relief.

It was five years ago that he received £2,000,000 from the sale of his Red Hackle whisky business and vowed that he would give it all away. He has kept his word.

Charities of every description have had their share. Glasgow Cathedral has been further beautified; Dunkeld Cathedral now rings out a glorious carillon which plays the favourite hymns of his late wife; Murrayfield has "underfloor" heating; a cool £35,000 has gone to his old school, Hillhead High for bursaries and sports ground improvements; Calderpark Zoo; the Scottish National Orchestra; the Burns Museum . . . there is no end to the list of benefactions.

But Mr Hepburn, a non-smoking teetotaller, is not in the

24

last stages of need. Only this week it was revealed that he was the man who paid 7,000 guineas for "The Start," an Alfred Munnings painting which shows Sir Gordon Richards at the start of a Newmarket race.

"I have enough to keep me comfortable here," he says, spreading an agile hand towards some 5,000 books and a magnificent collection of paintings by Munnings, Raeburn, Reynolds and many others in his elegant Glasgow home.

It has been a full life for the Army Captain, who came from Flanders Field with his £300 gratuity after the First World War and sank it into the business of blending whisky.

He told me a story which set the pattern of his charitable ways. During the First War a horse owner in Ayr was asked by the Army how much he wanted for his 32 animals. They were needed as officers' chargers.

"When he offered them for nothing, he was refused. It was against rules. So he charged 1s. each, saying that if his country needed them it was the least he could do to give them away. I decided that if he could do that, I could surely do something in the same spirit."

So Charles Hepburn gave away £2 million.

No wonder he beams humbly and happily with the air of a contented man. He came with nothing. He will go with not much more.

For the moment his greatest joy is that his wrists and legs can move again.

PILGRIMAGE TO
HOGMANAY HILL

—————————— *31st December 1964* ——————————

As the whisky flows and the fireside glows and the church
bells ring out the old I expect I shall take myself to the hill
tonight. For it has been a habit of mine on Hogmanay to
steal an hour of solitude, in the dying embers of a year, and
climb to the spot where I can look down again on the place
where I was born.

Call it a sentimental pilgrimage, for it is little more, but
it gives a man the chance to take stock of his life: to review
the journey so far and consider whether it is a path of progress
or decline.

The discovery is unlikely to be encouraging, for we are
poor mortals. But a gentle dose of self-examination once a
year does a man good. And what better time than Hogmanay, that incomparable milestone in the Scottish calendar?
What better place than where the journey began?

From there on Banks' Hill I can see the cottage of my
first light, the grass parks of first innocence and the track
which led me over the burn to the village school.

Down there lies the playground where we chased each
other at tackie or cock-fighting or cast a glance to the female
world of gym slip and skipping rope.

Then it was back to the Three Rs and the history dates and tales of faraway places; we were well-knit in a community of warmth and gaiety and sound principle, rooted in a place where our parents knew each other because they, too, had gone to school together; contended in the union of a common heritage.

From the hill I would watch great droves of horses come round the brae from Aikey Fair to be loaded on to trains at our railway junction.

Now there is no horse market and tomorrow the Beeching Axe will chop the railway livestock service, a vital part of life in a village which, for 100 years, has been the capital of the Aberdeenshire beef.

Remote men in far-off jungles decide our fate. Insidiously, they eat into the very fabric of our lives. But, thankfully, there is a solid rock of tradition in rural Scotland which will not readily surrender its standards nor bow to the slickness of a sophistication that is sometimes mistaken for progress.

The village of Maud is not what the world would call a beauty spot. But to me it is a thing more dear—a community of decent folk whose ways are the ways of true civilisation, a base from which I stepped out with joyous memory and to which I can happily return on such a night as this.

In the last of the light I will catch glimpse of the lovers' walk which accommodated the first stirrings of romance, the plans and the ploys and anticipation of the great wide world outside.

And now, as I eulogise on the places of my sunrise, with the maudlin call of a Hogmanay drunk echoing up the hill to my solitary perch and the folk singing their hymn of thanksgiving at a watchnight service, perhaps you would care to join me in a swig from the bottle—you with your thoughts, me with mine.

And together we can tread down the hill, back to the swirl

of life, glad for the mercies that have been, prayful for the things to come—and determined that our pilgrimage of 1965 will find no place for regrets.

FAR FROM THE
GLAMOUR OF WEMBLEY

——————— *10th April 1965* ———————

My thoughts are on football this April morning. Not just
on the inspiring spectacle of a Wembley international but
on the quieter slopes of Hampden Park, Glasgow. For it is
there that MY team will play this afternoon in the greatest
day in its history.

Peterhead Academy come south to battle it out with the
boys of Coatbridge St. Patrick's in the Scottish Schools Cup
Final.

It is the first time a team from the North-East has reached
this stage and for me it arouses a kaleidoscope of memory
which may have gained a good deal of colour since those
days in 1947 when I was streaking along the wing as
Peterhead Academy's outside-left.

A blissful smile spreads from my lips as I close my eyes
in recollection of the day I was first chosen for the team.

It was during a trial match and there I was, running down
the touchline and suddenly crossing a wildly speculative shot
into the goalmouth. Lo and behold! It beat everybody and
landed in the back of the net.

The players congratulated me. The gym master was
confident of a new Alan Morton and I walked away non-

chalantly, as if my fluke shot was a regular occurrence. So I was in the team.

The Morton magic never returned but I did have my moments. Perhaps my main asset as a footballer was my uncertainty. No back could feel confident about my next move. The fact which I have never admitted till now is that I was liable to do anything.

For example, as a keen student of the game. I became fascinated by the double shuffle. Night after night I practised it in the back garden till it was perfect.

It became my secret weapon on the field of play, guaranteed to baffle everybody—including myself.

And how could I forget that glorious moment when I came face to face with the right back of Banff Academy, who was supposed to be a clever fellow?

Clever, eh? I would show him. Picture the scene as I cantered up the field with the ease of Stanley Matthews. The back came in for the kill when suddenly I plunged into a spectacular body swerve. Nothing like it had ever been seen on a football field.

My opponent was so deceived that he ran one way. I was so deceived that I ran another. And the ball stayed exactly where it was!

It always puzzled me why a senior scout did not recognise that I could do a useful job for his team—like carrying the hamper, for example. But I was never spotted by anything more influential than a seagull.

It was enough, however, that I kept my place in the team. Indeed, no one dared remove me. For a combination of nuisance and entertainment values I was hard to beat.

Perhaps I was too much of a theorist. That there was football in my head was beyond doubt. It just refused to go to my feet.

Mind you, I played some wonderful games in my sleep.

And there I dreamed dreams of going to Hampden... dreams which would have come true if only I had been at Peterhead Academy now instead of 18 years ago.

But there is some consolation. Today's team will include two laddies from my own village of Maud who have followed the same route as myself, from the village school to the academy.

If they carry that cup back north tonight they will have helped to fulfil my boyhood desire. At Hampden today they will have the advantage of an extra man.

As an optimistic sucker for soccer I'll be out there in spirit, streaking up the left wing with all my former wizardry—and scoring goals that I'll speak about for years.

THE CROFTER'S SON WHO
GAVE SCOTLAND A VOICE

17th May 1965

For many years of youth I trod my native scene with little eye or ear for the things around me.

It was plain and familiar. People went about their work with steady gait in a life which seemed to have more drudgery than inspiration.

And then it happened. Within a matter of days the whole scene had gained new meaning, the plodding ploughman became the symbol of a deeper life, the land that lay so still began to yield more than crops and my heritage came alive.

At last my ears were opened to the voice of the land and for this I had to thank a man called Mitchell—James Leslie Mitchell, better known to the world as Lewis Grassic Gibbon.

I had just read his trilogy of novels called *The Scots Quair*, a remarkable piece of literature, which gets at the root of Scottish life and character and expresses it so that the whole English-speaking world can understand, while still retaining the native rhythms and essential flavour.

Mitchell was brought up, like myself, in the North-East of Scotland and knew the struggle and hardship of living on a croft. It roused rebellion in him but through the anger came the deeper love of the honest, decent folk who had to endure so much.

IIis headmaster, Alexander Gray, now retired in Stonehaven, showed me the essay which gave first hint of genius. The boy from the croft was only 12 years old when we wrote this:

> "*What an irresistible feeling of power comes when, on a calm clear night, you gaze up at the millions of glistening worlds and constellations which form the Milky Way.*
>
> "*'Tis then, and then only, that one can realise the full power of the Creator and the truth of the wild dream of the German poet. There is no beginning, yea, even as there is no end.*"

Home for Leslie Mitchell was a place of hard work and no books. Sons would follow their fathers on the soil and old man Mitchell was more than dumb-founded when the boy said he was going to write for a living. Fegs, it was hardly decent!

But the course was set, and I wonder with what pride his father would have read a recent Higher English paper in the Scottish Leaving Certificate which said: "Write a critical account of the treatment of Scottish life in the novels of Scott or Stevenson, or Lewis Grassic Gibbon."

There is the measure of the man.

His writings have become compulsory reading in many Scottish schools, and soon we are to have the first biography of the man. Ian Munro, the Glasgow writer and dramatist, who is now a lecturer at Aberdeen College of Education, is the author, and the publishers have it scheduled for later this year.

Grassic Gibbon wrote 15 books, culminating in the famous trilogy. He was already the friend of men like H. G. Wells and was starting to make his way as a financial success. In the summer of 1934 he came north in his first motor car, which symbolised his progress.

But father Mitchell was not impressed. He had never reconciled himself to the fact of his son's genius. Not, that is, until 1935 when he suddenly became aware that he had probably sired the greatest Scottish writer of the century.

His intentions had been good. And his tears were of the honest variety when the "loon" who had gone away from the land of his fathers came home to rest in the kirkyard of Arbuthnott.

Wracked by stomach pains, he had gone for an operation—and did not rally. At 34 a great light was dimmed for ever. Grassic Gibbon was one of a breed of North-East writers whose early struggles seemed to burn up their resources and leave them scarce of manhood.

With Alexander Gray, the dominie who gave him books and guided his early years, I went to the kirkyard where his ashes lie.

We read the words on the headstone: "The kindness of friends; the warmth of toil; the peace of rest"—words from that closing passage of *Sunset Song* which can move a man to tears.

From Grassic Gibbon's own place of the sunset, Mr Gray turned his gaze across the steaming soil of the Mearns, with its parks and its peesies, the folk still working their crofts, and the hills beyond.

The voice that had spoken for them all was a voice that echoed from the forest days of the Maglemosians, down through time to the 1960's. It was the voice of Aul' Scotia, timeless and enduring.

For Mr Gray, it was the very special voice of a pupil.

HE SET A NEW TREND
AT IBROX

———————— *26th May 1965* ————————

In a flourish of 90,000 crisp pound notes, James Baxter, the pit boy from Fife who rose to fame as a footballer of world class, departs the Scottish scene, perhaps for ever.

From the bastions of Ibrox Park the man who has been the stormy petrel of Scottish football for several years moves to the wealth of Roker Park, Sunderland.

There—who knows?—he may take over the mantle of another famous Scot, Hughie Gallacher, who was the idolised toast of Newcastle and North-East England a generation ago.

Behind, he leaves a trail of memory that will make its mark on the minds of football supporters throughout his native land.

When the dust has settled we shall remember ball playing Baxter the Brilliant . . . Baxter the Rebel . . . but, most of all, I suspect, Baxter the Individualist.

The truth is that Baxter set a new trend in the image of a Rangers player. In an age when youth was asserting itself, with unprecedented vigour, he withheld himself from total absorption in the great tradition of the mighty Rangers.

While great Rangers of the past—men of the stature of

George Young—were Rangers first and themselves for what was left, the man from Fife remained Jim Baxter in all his shades.

Not all the funnelling of tradition through the true-blue filters of Scot Symon, the manager, Davie Kinnear, the trainer, Alan Morton, the director, could change the flame-coloured personality of the boy who knew the darkness of the pits.

It expressed itself in various ways, not least in his determined stand for what he considered to be his rights.

Within two years of his transfer from Raith Rovers to Rangers, he was holding out for better terms in a way that no new boy might previously have dared.

By December of that same year—1962—he was asking for a transfer. "I just want a change of club," he said. And the uncertainty has continued since then.

The most rabid Rangers supporter has never been able to relax, feeling that Jim was really here to stay. There has always been the doubt. Always something liable to happen.

Then he became captain and was leading his team to European glory when he broke his leg in Vienna. Rangers slid back, and the Baxter spirits too.

It was the final impetus towards the final departure. And now Jim goes, only weeks before his wedding on June 16 to pretty Jean Ferguson from Coatbridge.

The joy of Sunderland this morning will echo as sadness in many parts of Scotland. Jim has meant many things to many people.

We shall all remember with pleasure the silken touches of his football art which are all too rarely seen today. We shall see them now only when he plays for Scotland at Hampden, as he surely must again.

Beyond that, it's just "Thanks for the memory."

AS BIG JOHN BOWS OUT

*He's the Front Row Forward Who Hasn't Been
On The Winning Side For 20 Years*

─────── ─────── *2nd August 1965* ───────────

The fine physique of John Macdonald Bannerman, enhanced
by swinging kilt and bushy eyebrows, embodies in many
ways the spirit of Scotland.

Whether winning a gold medal at the Mod, captaining
Scotland as a front row forward on the Rugby field or rasping
out the pleas of an oft-forgotten people, he has borne the
authentic stamp of his native heath.

Yet the voice which has been raised in all corners of the
earth has never been heard in the place where it would have
gained most attention—the Palace of Westminster.

Eight times in 20 years Bannerman fought the Liberal
cause in parliamentary elections. Eight times without success. Now he has decided that he will not stand again. And
yesterday in his home near Loch Lomond he talked very
frankly about the years in which he has fought the good fight
for the sake of Scotland.

"There is no romance in politics," he told me. "I have
found it to be a dirty game in which the worst of human
attributes begin to show. If you try to play it cleanly, it is
not easy.

"Yet, each defeat inspired me to keep on trying, not only

37

because of my belief in Liberalism but because, when one is fouled in a game, one does not retreat. One simply fights harder." The sportsman was talking.

I believe that, ironically, it was the very strength of Bannerman which kept him out of Parliament. There is a clue to this paradox in his own words.

"Whenever they saw me coming in an election, Tories and Socialists would stand shoulder to shoulder. It was as if they got together and said: 'Whatever else happens, it must not be the Liberal who wins here.' "

He was chairman of the Scottish Liberals and four of his elections were at Inverness. Gradually he pushed Labour into third place and in 1955 lost to the Tory by only 966 votes.

He later moved to Paisley—and, alas, it was then that his successor at Inverness GAINED the seat for the Liberals.

But Bannerman was delighted. For he is a man who burns the flame of Scotland in his breast. If he had sought personal glory at Westminster, he could have had it at the beginning of the war when he had the chance to be National Liberal candidate for Argyll. Virtually, he says, that would have made him a Tory member—and that would never have done.

Descended from men who were burned out in the Clearances John Bannerman is a ready-made enemy of the Highland landlord.

"I have always known that the land was the basis on which the Highland people lived and that, unless they had reasonable access to it, they could not progress. I merely wanted the owners to become the trustees of the land for the people.

"The future of the Highlands rests in the use of the land. If you own the land there, you also own the law and the destiny of the people. The result has been the decimation of the people and a misuse of the land."

John Bannerman seeks an elevation of our economy and our culture. When his family moved from South Uist to

Glasgow, they brought with them the solid standards of the croft.

"It was a Glasgow house but it was a Gaelic home," he recalls. His father started as a telegraphist in the Post Office in Glasgow and became superintendent.

Young John started at Shawlands Academy and reached Balliol College, Oxford. Among his many honours he was later to become Lord Rector of Aberdeen University.

He stands out as a distinguished Scot, combining in his personality an echo of history, an awareness of the present—and a vision of the future. He might go down, alas, as the greatest politician Scotland never had.

MY FRIEND DOD, AND THE
CATASTROPHE OF LOVE

My friend Dod from the Hill of Culsh is sorely perturbed.
As if the summer were not bad enough and the harvest a
good deal worse, an event of this week is topping them all
for catastrophic happenings.

His fellow-bachelor, Willie Taylor, from the village of
New Deer, is about to commit the unpardonable sin of
getting married.

Now Willie is one of a bevy of eligible gentlemen in the
Aberdeenshire village which takes a little pride in being the
bastion of bachelordom.

Forty or more of them stand shoulder to shoulder in a
population of a few hundred, resisting with musketeering
solidarity any hint of romantic overture.

But every now and then, alas, there is a traitor. Dod finds
it hard to understand. In a warm summer he blames the heat
but more often resigns himself to the unpredictability of
human behaviour.

Dod and his friends are all the more surprising because
they are overflowing with masculinity.

They are dour, down-to-earth chaps, whose forebears
spent the last 200 years struggling to turn sour scrubland

into productive acres. Now that they have succeeded they are not going to be put off balance by the fickleness of a woman.

Several times I have chided Dod about the advantages of having a wife. I have carefully avoided romantic allusion least it should scunner him, concentrating instead on the purely practical.

"Just look at the comfort of it all," I would say, feeling that I had him half-way down the aisle.

"Comfort?" he would grunt. "If it's comfort ye're offerin', I would rather hae my lang drawers. They keep ye warm at nicht—and ye can change them when ye want."

So that would be that. Were Dod ever to contemplate matrimony it would be as a farmer considers his stock. Her shell-like ears and soft brown eyes would pass for nothing if her pedigree and yield potential were suspect.

The women of his district are seldom embarrassed by any outward expression of love and affection because they seldom get it.

But the fact that the parish population shows no sign of decreasing is clear enough evidence that love—and womanly guile—will eventually find a way.

They land their man all right. Even if he has to be hauled down the aisle in a halter, he goes the way of all flesh.

Willie Taylor, this week's groom, is quoted as saying: "It happens to us all."

With such resignation and fortitude, I think we can safely leave the affairs of nature to take their course. Dod and his co-celibates of rural Scotland may not be God's gift to romance.

But, damn it man, they are dependable!

I MARRIED EDEN

But Gardening Was Never My Strong Point

——————— *11th November 1965* ———————

By the process of natural selection I went to church one day to marry a girl called Eden. And in the life that followed, there came a house and a garden.

And in the garden there came little green things which grew into big green things and this abundance of greenery was variously described as weeds, weeds, and more weeds.

Eden refuses to be associated with the wilderness. Indeed, had this been the original Garden of Eden, the whole course of human history would almost certainly have been changed. It is doubtful if Adam would ever have found his Eve!

No. This is the Garden of Jack, a man with a rural background and a deep-rooted regard for life in the countryside but a lamentable ignorance of the things that grow.

And the reason that I tell of it now is that, contrary to all sense and accepted practice, this is the beginning of my gardening season.

It is now, in soggy, dead November that you find me out there with spade or graip, digging viciously into soil which defied me in the spring-time but cannot raise a paltry weed in winter.

This is the only season when I can win. I dig over great

drills of soil in the sure and certain knowledge that nothing sinister will happen behind my back overnight.

In the morning you will find me out there full of confidence, triumphant foot resting on indifferent spade and a challenging voice addressing the soil with such rasping rhetoric as "Well, whaur's your damned weeds now?"

It will continue until the snows come. And when springtime raises an ugly head again I shall probably spread an abundance of weed-killer and retire to hibernation until the autumn, when I shall once more sally forth with a "Heigh!" and a "Ho!"

But it has not always been so. In the early days, I made an earnest effort to be a gardener. The results, however, were so disappointing—and even mystifying—that I have been advised to write a book about them.

I could call it "Greenfinger" and would guarantee it to become one of the most baffling whodunits of all time. Take, for instance, the Case of the Missing Potatoes. What a chapter that would make!

It began when I first acquired a garden of my own and set about providing my family with the staple foods of life. Having been reared on a philosophy of "Meal, milk and tatties", I had already bought a barrel of meal and tied an old cow to the clothes pole. Now for the tatties.

"Dig a trench," said the pundits, so I excavated with diligence. Then I flung dung to the bottom, replaced a layer of earth and planted my potatoes.

That was two years ago and I haven't seen them since. Some said I planted them upside down so I bought the Australian papers for a few months but they never showed a shaw there either.

Others said the soil needed lime so that was applied with liberality. Lime? For all the difference it made I might as well have poured on the lager.

The lettuce had a comparable fate but in that I had the consolation of a special award from the Loyal Order of Rabbits—for The Man Least Likely To Succeed.

But now we come to the saddest part. Once upon a time this travesty of a garden was the showpiece of the district. That was when roses abounded. That was when there was not a self-respecting weed in sight. That was when the previous owner was there.

People came from far and near to gaze in disbelief at this floral splendour. It was a sort of Mecca. It still is, mind you. Now I just show the pilgrims how to Mecca-mess of it.

Apart from weeds, however, I would modestly claim that I am a dab hand at growing rhubarb. And this year, as if in defiance of all those miserable experiences, I have a trump card up my sleeve.

This year I will be carrying out an experiment which will bring long-nosed scientists from all corners of the globe to peer through their pince-nez spectacles and then to screech with delight when I succeed.

Plainly, folks, I am going to plant a feather in the much-cherished hope that a hen will grow.

HAME WI' MY AIN FOLK

*And Where Better To Recap On
The Journey Through Life?*

―――――――――― *12th April 1966* ――――――――――

The prophet hath no honour in his own land—or so they say. But without being much of a prophet, I can sit down today to deny it.

For I have just had an experience that was both humbling and inspiring, back in the land of Aberdeenshire where I belong.

The journey north to the village of Maud was in answer to a request to appear in the local church—face to face with the minister, the Rev David McBride, who makes a speciality of celebrity interviews.

And there was I, parading through from the vestry to the full glare of the parish to take my place before the pews where once I sat as an innocent Sunday school boy, pondering the inscription above the pulpit: "This is none other but the House of God."

Now I could sense a warming glow flooding up to where I sat; warm country folk who knew me as a child and were back to see how much I had made of life.

For, whatever reason, there was an air of quiet pride, as if the local boy had possibly made good.

Even if I had been so disposed, there would have been

45

little chance of putting on the agony here.

For out there was the woman who ran to the cattle mart to tell my father that I was born.

He was in the auctioneer's rostrum at the time and casually absorbed the information between selling a long-legged piner and a rough Irish stirk.

Out there, too, were the teacher who guided my infant years at Maud School, the boy who was my faithful pal through thick and thin, the girl who stirred in me the early pangs of feeling.

Here were so many of the pillars of reference that are essential to the foundation of a satisfactory life.

And the minister began by reading an essay which I once wrote, a eulogy on the place and the people who formed the pattern of permanency that gave us roots and a settled outlook on life.

Then he reversed my normal routine and subjected me to interview, quizzing on a variety of subjects from religion to objectionable television programmes.

My views on youth? There seemed to be an awful lot of them and their main lack seemed to be a grounding in childhood. But there was a good deal to be said for them.

And we sang a hymn and the minister read another essay in which I recalled the men who went away from our village scene in 1939, and did not come back.

I am told it was a moving experience and the gratitude of my ain folk was expressed in a firm handshake at the church door as they left.

It does a man good from time to time to seek again those reference points of his early days. I come again refreshed for the daily task.

SLOWLY, SCOTLAND BEGINS TO
RECOGNISE THIS TRAGIC GENIUS

———————— *25th May 1966* ————————

Shortly after he wrote *Sunset Song* in 1932, Lewis Grassic Gibbon paid a return visit to the North-East of Scotland, where he belonged. And there, as he arrived at his father's croft at Bloomfield, Arbuthnott, he was met by his mother who looked at him sadly and said: "Laddie, what did you want to write all that muck for? It's the speak of the place. Your father's fair affronted and I'm ashamed of you."

Gibbon never quite got over the deep hurt of that moment. For the "muck" was his great masterpiece, the triumph which was to raise him to an immortal place in Scottish literature, bracketed with people like Sir Walter Scott, acclaimed and envied by writers everywhere and read throughout the world.

By February, 1935—a week before his 34th birthday—Gibbon was dead. Today his biography is published, written by a Glaswegian, Ian S. Munro, who significantly perhaps, has been drawn to live in the North-East.

Sunset Song was a story of the writer's own parish near Stonehaven, of the toil and the drudgery of the land and the men and women who were of it.

George Malcolm Thomson was inspired to write: "This

is the real Scotland at last . . . it seems to me the pioneer of something new and very interesting in Scottish letters. Perhaps the first really Scottish novel."

Here, in fact, was poetry in prose, the poetry of the land; the soil itself was speaking with eloquence and those who read were excited.

Here, indeed, was something new, the first of three such novels written in a unique style and later to be produced under one cover with the title *A Scots Quair*.

Gibbon's real name was Leslie Mitchell (his later pen-name came from his mother's maiden name of Lilias Grassic Gibbon) son of decent, country folk who came across from Aberdeenshire to scratch a living from a few acres of the red-clay soil of the Mearns.

At Arbuthnott School, young Mitchell was the odd laddie, the one who read books in the playground and on his bicycle (once landing in the ditch as a result!).

But the dominie, Alexander Gray, who is still hale and hearty in Stonehaven, spotted the talent and encouraged it.

Mitchell later went to Mackie Academy, Stonehaven, but the rebel in him was emerging and he fell foul of teachers, leaving without honour.

He tried journalism in Aberdeen and Glasgow but left the profession under a cloud. So he joined the RAF went to the Middle East and found scope for his interest in ancient civilisation.

His later writings on the subject astonished the learned.

He rode the desert on a camel, dreaming dreams of the Golden Age of man and standing stoutly for the belief that prehistoric man was a well-behaved creature, ruined only by the coming of "civilisation".

Then the novels began to roll. In the last seven years of his tragically short life he wrote 17 volumes. He was fascinated by time and space and became the friend of H. G.

Wells, who was an admirer.

Recognition had been so slow that he found it difficult, once he was established, to turn down a commission. North-East writers, alas, have a sad history of burning themselves up in furious activity.

In the summer of 1934, Gibbon came north from his home in Welwyn Garden City to visit the old places. By now he had a motor car and he took his parents for runs.

By now, too, his bitterness about their attitude had turned more to an understanding of their own hard struggle in life. But they yielded little in their dour opposition.

He spent a few days with his old headmaster, Mr Gray, and while there wrote the last words of his *Scots Quair*.

A few months later stomach trouble was draining him and he failed to rally from an operation. They buried his ashes in Arbuthnott Kirkyard, in the soil of his seeding, in the company of his ain folk, some of whom had been portrayed—and not always with flattery—in his writings.

We are often slow to recognise our own. In this scientific century, we Scots have produced one of the great literary minds and too many of us are scarcely aware of it.

They are beginning to read him in the schools and now Ian Munro brings us closer to the great warmth and humanity of the man.

For my part, he aroused in me an awareness of my heritage, a reappraising of my roots and a new joy in being a Scot. How could I withhold my gratitude?

THE SOMME—THE HORROR
OF JULY 1ST 1916

Fifty Years Ago Today

─────────── *1st July 1966* ───────────

They called it the Battle of the Somme. But they might have called it the bloodiest episode in the history of mankind.

For the frightful carnage and destruction of that battle—which began 50 years ago today—is almost unequalled.

What began on July 1, 1916, as the Big Push to drive the Germans from their strongholds on the ridges overlooking the River Somme, was still being fought nearly five months later. The gain—five miles.

In those five miles more than a million British, French, and German soldiers were killed or wounded in a stinking wilderness of water and mud.

Yet the official bulletins hailed it as a great victory. A wedge had been driven into the German ranks. The courage of the British P.B.I. (Poor Bloody Infantry, as they called themselves) is said to have broken the heart of the great professional German Army, eventually leading to its retreat.

Well, there may be a case for saying it was the beginning of the end of the First World War. But what a costly victory! What a way to win a war!

In Scottish homes, as elsewhere in the kingdom, the dreaded telegram had brought its own tragic message.

For they were there, our men—Scots Guards, KOSB, Royal Scots, Black Watch, Royal Scots Fusiliers, HLI, Gordons, Seaforths, Argylls, Camerons and Cameronians (Scottish Rifles).

So what was the Somme all about? Where did it go wrong?

The First World War had been running for nearly two years and in 1915 there had been failure to break through the German lines.

A new army was being raised at home, mostly volunteers and largely the better type of young man so far as physique, brains and education were concerned.

It was obvious that a massive offensive was being prepared. It came in the fertile valley of the Somme, in the picturesque lands of Picardy, Northern France, on that morning of July 1, 1916.

The Germans had held the high ground for more than 18 months, dug into positions they considered impregnable.

The British divisions moved up to the area, with French support on the right, ready to attack on a 20-mile front.

It is June 30 and the scene is set—a scene where nightingales and larks still sing, and the poppy blooms.

In the night hours before the battle, the troops move out of their billets in cottages, barns and byres to the trenches. The songs and jokes are over for now.

Then the shelling is resumed—a bombardment which has gone on for night after night, and which, the generals believe, will so devastate the Germans that the infantry will not meet much opposition.

The final bombardment begins at 6.30am across the hundreds of yards of no-man's-land, turning the sun to a dull red glow in the dust and smoke.

The guns lift an hour later, as the sun is rising clear in the eastern sky. The battle is on.

Our soldiers, some swearing and shouting to escape their

own fear, are over the top of the trenches into battle.

But their sandbag parapets are already spurting with German bullets. A mass of enemy shells is bursting among the advancing lines of British soldiers and a German eye-witness later describes it:

"Whole sections seemed to fall—all along the line men could be seen throwing up their arms and collapsing, never to move again."

So what went wrong? Of all the significant information sent back before the battle by officers probing the strength and lay-out of the enemy, no one seems to have reported that the Germans were beautifully entrenched in dug-outs 30 feet deep in solid chalk.

Then they clambered up steep shafts, and pulled out the machine guns and swept no-man's-land with a hail of bullets.

Our men, who had advanced in close-packed waves, kept stepping out to certain death till few were left standing. In pathetic twos and threes the survivors struggled back.

After the main offensive there followed months of trench warfare, men living like animals, sometimes thigh-deep in water. Meals were half-cooked, often raw.

Men went mad in the rat-infested trenches.

Field-Marshal Sir Douglas Haig was much criticised. He had commanded from well behind, sending fresh troops to fill the gaps, apparently with little idea of how hopeless was their task.

At home, Scots folk bore their sorrow with the courage that befitted the sons and husbands who went away.

They were the cream of a generation these men who died, and there is little doubt that we have been the poorer because they did not live to father children of their own stamp. The human stock may take some time to restore its quality.

Meantime, whatever the folly of the planning, we should

not forget our debt to these fine men.

At the going down of the sun and in the morning—especially this July morning—let us remember them.

SO THIS IS LIFE AT
THE HALF-WAY MARK!

———————— *9th July 1966* ————————

I gave myself a special survey in the shaving mirror yesterday and considered what it was like to be 35. Thirty-five? The very sound of it was anything but sweet music on a birthday morning.

Yet this confrontation with myself was an interesting exercise. The vision in the mirror, I felt, could well have been someone else.

It was as if I had projected myself beyond the body confines and was viewing the creature with an objective eye. What I saw looked all of 35.

Those boyish creases had cemented into shallow furrows which would, in turn, become the wrinkled lines of time.

The hair which had once been so thick as to be embarrassing had dispersed itself to the four winds, except for a scattering of loyal strands.

From between the eyes emerged a nose which began on a mistaken course and curved back to something short of beautiful. Yet it had been my nose for 35 years and it blows quite satisfactorily.

The general contour of the face, I decided, was much as I had always remembered it, neither fatter nor thinner, just older.

So there was the body, detached as if it might possibly not belong.

But the spirit was different. I still viewed life from the standpoint of 18. Well . . . at a stretch I could see myself with the 23 year olds, but not a day beyond. And don't we all?

To this day, I can assess someone as "thirty, if a day", and feel that they can give me a few years. I have interviewed people in important positions and accorded them the respect of their years—only to find that they are younger than me!

It seems only yesterday that I envied Ronnie Simpson when he was the schoolboy star of Queen's Park Football Club. We were about the same age.

Today the fact that he is still a star is a wonder to many people—because he is an old man in the game.

An old man—at my age! Yet that was my own judgment on my father when he was 35, a solid captain in the L.D.V., preparing a dreadful fate for the Germans if they happened to penetrate to our small village.

The trouble with being 35 is that you are neither young nor middle-aged. When I suggested to some more mature colleagues yesterday that I was mid-way through the allotted span, they exploded.

In their fighting fifties, they clearly considered that *they* were the ones approaching the half-way house. A fine testimony to the optimism and immortal outlook of we struggling mortals!

So perhaps I should content myself with those 35 years and feel glad that I have clear memories of King George V's Jubilee, the Spanish Revolution and those golden summers which used to shine before 1939.

Not forgetting that the best is yet to come—if life really begins at 40.

THE DAY I WAS PROUD
TO CHEER ON ENGLAND!

London on Saturday night was a heady experience. It was like V.E. night all over again.

And there I was, a loyal Scot, joining in England's celebration of the World Cup triumph I had seen explode into ecstasy on Wembley's emotion-charged terraces as that epic game ended.

Outside the Royal Garden Hotel in Kensington, the crowd cheered and roared.

Inside, in an atmosphere of gay abandon, the English team was dining with the other semi-finalists, as the guests of FIFA, breaking off to show the Cup from the balcony.

Everybody was a friend.

I was in the banquet hall when the company returned for the speeches. I had no invitation, but on this crazy night, who cared?

The Prime Minister [Harold Wilson] was there, fresh from his American talks.

He heard my accent and wanted to know what part of Scotland I came from. We shook hands on England's victory.

George Brown, the Economics Minister, was in great form, telling me how West Ham had won the World Cup.

West Ham? Well, Bobby Moore of West Ham was the English captain, and all the scorers came from West Ham. So who was going to argue?

Then it was presentation time. The orchestra played the national music of the player being honoured.

There was the balalaika as Lev Yashin of Russia received his award as best goalkeeper.

As Bobby Moore got several awards, George Brown leapt to his feet and led the orchestra into West Ham's own song, "I'm Forever Blowing Bubbles".

When it began to break up in the early hours, nobody wanted to go.

I walked to my hotel, glad for once to be an English supporter, and feeling that a memorable occasion left only one possible improvement—if Scotland had won the World Cup.

WHY THESE SISTERS
ARE TOAST OF A VILLAGE

—————————— *29th August 1966* ——————————

As the corn rustled in the calm of a Victorian summer, little Bell Duncan went up the dusty road for her first day as a pupil at the village school.

It was *her* village and *her* heritage. The place was Maud, in Aberdeenshire. The year: 1888.

Fifty years on . . . and I was taking the tarmacadam route to the village school, there to be taught the fundamentals of education by none other than Bell Duncan, who had not moved from the place of her birth. That was in the late thirties.

And next month—a further 30 years on—the village who owes her so much is giving a complimentary dinner. But it is not for Bell alone.

Her sister Jessie recently gave up after 46 years as a teacher, nearly half of them spent in her native village.

Together they will be honoured—and how well they deserve it.

For they represent that passing breed of pupil-teachers, that race of conscientious people who learned their craft the hard way and rose to become the backbone of our Scottish educational system.

How well I remember their firm but kindly coaxing, the smell of their chalk and inkwells and fresh-cut exercise books. There was no nonsense in their uncomplicated world of the Three Rs but a caramel of reward on a Friday afternoon.

It was a pleasure to speak again to Miss Bell Duncan yesterday, to hear the Buchan ring of an accent which has remained unchanged in a changing world.

She talked of the humour.

"There's a middle-aged man I know whose name I never hear but I remember the day he came to Maud School. All day he sat in that infant room just gazing up at the ventilator grill.

"At the end of the day, when asked what he had been looking at, he replied with a question: 'Are ye ill wi' rottens?' which, translated into English means 'Are you troubled with rats?' "

Clearly this farmer's boy was more interested in rodent infestation than education!

There was the day that Miss Duncan was giving her class a lesson on children's pets. One boy announced that his dog was called Moreover and when she expressed doubts about such a name the little chap assured her of his authority.

"Ay, Miss, it says it in the Bible—'Moreover the dog came and licked his sores.' "

The two Miss Duncans find it hard to understand why they should be honoured with a dinner and presentation. Perhaps it is not for them to see the service which they have rendered.

Perhaps they have taken for granted the fact that by their efforts and example they laid the sure foundation to countless hundreds of lives.

Their interest was real and their concern deep.

The original Maud School, to which Miss Bell Duncan first went in 1888, survived to become the village smiddy. But even that has had its day and now it stands derelict on the Honeyneuk corner.

Bell Duncan has lived through it all. And, with sister Jessie, has lived to earn the gratitude of many people.

LONG JOHNS!

————————— *9th November 1966* —————————

It was the cold snap that did it. There I was, rummaging in a trunk and dreaming dreams of a warmth and comfort which have eluded me since that ill-advised day, some years ago, when I discarded my Long Johns.

I had been caught up, I fear, in the astonishing prejudice which exists against this most sensible and versatile of all anatomical coverings.

But why—can someone tell me why—do people laugh at long drawers?

It is one of those instinctive reactions which seems to defy all reason. Because where else will you find such comfort and protection?

I first encountered Long Johns long ago in the country, where the cold is a greater problem. Every clothes line had at least one pair, blowing horizontally of a Monday morning in full-bottomed glory.

Adult men around me wore them, lived with them, worked with them, danced with them, and died and were buried with them, sometimes the same pair, folk said, and that was as fine a tribute to thrift and durability as I can imagine.

LONG JOHNS

While city folks shivered about windy streets, with eddying gusts quivering their suspenders, my rural kinsmen faced the howling gales with a brand of central heating which the gas and electricity and oil-fired men have yet to match.

As I remember it in our matter-of-fact country scene, it was counted soft to wear pyjamas. Nearly as bad, in fact, as talking English and pretending you were somebody.

So fathers and grandfathers slept in their long drawers— and usually their shirts as well.

As a boy in the thirties, I thought I belonged to a generation which was going to do away with such old-fashioned nonsense, opting instead for the smarter city styles.

But in the hard freeze of a particular winter I secretly took to the traditional garb and realised that there was a lot to be said for the establishment after all! I have never felt better.

Of course there were awkward moments when, say, at an elimination dance, you had to roll up a trouser leg. It took a well-practised movement to roll the leg of your drawers at the same time.

It was an odd sight, too, if you tried to wear them with the kilt!

Nevertheless, I wore them and wore them and stood at the altar on my wedding day in unsurpassed comfort.

While the minister blessed the bride, I blessed my long drawers, for it happened to be the coldest day of the century and there was no heating in that spacious kirk.

Sooner than later, however, I fell victim of the prejudice which can persist against sensible things. I discarded them and have not taken to them for several years.

But I have no doubt that, as time goes by and winters grow colder, I shall turn again to my woollen wonders.

Then, by George, with such renewal of warmth and confidence, I'll see the pants off most people!

A SOFT SPOT
FOR THE TRAMS

There was a major ticket scramble in Glasgow last night which had nothing to do with that football match at Celtic Park.

It involved people who were desperately keen to see a film show about trams.

From Dalmuir to Auchenshuggle they rolled in by the score, filling the Scottish Film Council's cinema at Charing Cross and overflowing to another hall.

They saw a programme which included the Scottish premiere of Kevin Brownlow's film on the last of the Glasgow trams, which he calls "Nine Dalmuir West".

There were also fragments tracing the history of the tram from the horse-drawn days through electrification to that tearful farewell in Glasgow in 1962.

Aberdeen, Dundee and Edinburgh had already disposed of their fleets.

Mr John Huntley of the British Film Institute talked of this new fascination with the immediate past.

"There is this interest in the music hall, in steam loco-motives, in tram cars," he said. "Do you know there are now three societies devoted to the preservation of cinema organs?

"With older people it is probably nostalgia but a large part of the interest comes from the young, who are finding it hard to imagine, for example, what it must have been like to have tram cars trundling along Sauchiehall Street or Argyle Street."

Today, the Golden Mile at Blackpool is the only place in Britain where the tram car still runs and even there it has a certain museum quality about it.

Of course, it hogged the middle of the road and slowed up traffic; it was costly. But the heart had a special corner for the old tram.

The clank-clank of the bell, the hiss of the brakes, the sway and lurch of the old thing itself, not to mention the repartee of the conductors, founded a folklore.

The stories were legion and they came more often than not from Glasgow.

The conductress who shouted "Come oan, get aff!" is now a legend.

And the hefty one who followed the energetic passenger upstairs and right to the front of the empty tram to ask breathlessly and sourly: "What stoaped ye?"

There is already an old-fashioned look about the situation in one of Mr Huntley's films, recording the last of Aberdeen's trams hurtling into a funeral pyre on the Links in 1958.

Two figures are holding grimly to the rail, jumping clear only at the last minute.

One of them is me—the young reporter not only getting a story but establishing a claim to being the last person ever to travel on an Aberdeen tram car.

Just one of the daft things you want to be able to tell your grandchildren.

Nine years earlier, this was my report of that bizarre scene in Aberdeen, when I was late-night reporter on *The Press & Journal*.

LAST OF THE TRAMS
GO UP IN SMOKE

Perhaps it's a lot of sentimental nonsense, but I'll be glad to tell my grandchildren I was the last passenger to travel on an Aberdeen tramcar.

It happened early this morning when the city bade the last of its trams a sad farewell.

Unannounced, the remaining eighteen were driven from the King Street depot to Castle Street and were then pushed by lorry to the tram track at the Beach where they were set alight.

As word spread that the great cremation was "on", crowds rushed to watch the blaze.

Sixteen trams were already blazing when the last two were lined up for the final push into the inferno.

The lorry started the big push and as Car No 20 hurtled to its death I could not resist the temptation to run alongside, jump on and then jump off, seconds before it went up in flames.

Pyjama-clad householders were among the hundreds who watched the blaze. And many people came by car.

Cameras clicked at every angle as Pressmen, newsreel men and amateurs with box cameras recorded the closing chapter.

"It's a shame . . . It's a disgrace", were among the comments of the onlookers.

"Damn it, man, ye aye kent far the trammie wis gaun— it hid tae follow the rails," said one old resident who now finds difficulty with the buses.

Among those present were an enthusiastic band of young tram-spotters.

One of them, Alexander Forsyth, a C.A. apprentice, said he had mixed feelings about the going of the trams.

Another keen youngster, who managed to rip off a souvenir was seventeen-year-old Grammar School boy, Ian Halliday.

Supervising delivery of the trams to the Beach were Chief Inspector Gove and Mr James Mackie, rolling stock superintendent of the transport department.

Among the spectators were Louis Argo (43), Roslin Street, and Allan Bannerman (25), Menzies Road, both tram drivers.

TROUBLE WITH
THE MINI-SKIRT

————————— *17th May 1967* —————————

Angela Cash flies into Scotland to add her measured tones to one of the pressing international problems of the day. It is a subject which has already drawn pronouncements from many lands.

In China, it is condemned as an open defiance of Mao Tse-tung's thoughts; in Zambia it is deplored as a symbol of Right-wing colonialism; in Tunisia it is a badge of Left-wing revolt.

In short (very short), it is the mini-skirt—that paradox of the quantity laws which proves that the less you buy, the more you have to show for it.

In the progression from mini to micro-mini to skini-mini we have arrived at a state of indiscriminate shrinkage where any young thing, whether she measures 36-24-36 or a straight-forward five-by-five, is displaying her uprights with scant regard for the quality of the goods.

According to fashion designer Miss Cash, only six per cent of Scots girls are wearing minis, compared to 24 per cent in London. I would guess that her figures are more short than revealing.

But more interesting is the fact that we are all talking

about it.

The girls themselves are claiming that the mini-skirt gives them more freedom to walk, that it gives them the appearance of height; they will tell you anything, in fact, except the more likely story that it draws attention to their anatomies and puts them right in fashion.

There was a time in those distant days of Victoria when the leg was never seen at all, to expose an ankle would have been described by Papa as the liberty of a hussy.

The female form was such a mystery to the average male that there were little boys who grew up with the notion that crinoline ladies were actually shaped that way.

In more recent times, the knee-cap has become the starting point for arguments about modesty and decency.

It was there, in my not-so-distant youth, that the female leg used to disappear into the realms of mystery to follow its course to the torso by routes which were only imagined.

What lay beyond the veils may have the tenderness of a twig or the fleshiness of a Friesian.

The unknown played its part in nature's design and was part of a woman's charm.

But the curtain went up and now we are being given the full, unexpurgated story, in all its disappointments. What used to be stimulating is nothing more than commonplace.

And that, I hasten to add, is not just the view of this self-appointed connoisseur but of almost every single male I consulted on the matter.

The manufacturers, charging no less for much less, are in love with the mini-Winnies.

But let us not despair. There is a limit to exposure if you are not to catch pneumonia—or be caught by the police.

I predict that the hemline will settle back at about three or four inches above the knee ere long. That's where men like it.

MINI-SKIRTS

On that day it will no longer be possible to be "with it" if you are without it.

WHY I'M GLAD MY GRANNY
HAD THIS NIGHT OUT

———————— *5th August 1967* ————————

When Scotland's new orchestra, the Northern Philharmonic, made its debut in Aberdeen last night the programme included, appropriately, the famous Grieg Piano Concerto.

Appropriately, because Grieg's paternal roots are all in the North-East of Scotland and indeed if his grandfather had not made the mistake of emigrating to Norway some time after the Jacobite Rebellion he might have been the national composer of Scotland instead of Norway.

Be that as it may, I am delighted that my granny was there at the Music Hall, Aberdeen, last night. She deserved her night out. In fact, they made her guest of honour—and who better?

She is a close relative of Edvard Grieg, descended from that same Greig family (note the composer's change of spelling) which had its home in the Fraserburgh-Rathen-Inverallochy corner of Aberdeenshire.

It was there that Edvard Grieg's grandfather acted as Norwegian Consul and from there that that branch of the family set out for a new life across the North Sea.

From those who stayed there came people like my grandmother, Mrs Edith Barron, who grew up as Edith Greig,

70

daughter of Gavin Greig, himself a brilliant scholar and pianist and no mean composer and playwright.

We are what is commonly called "a musical family", and I say this in some kind of reply to the many Norwegians who declare that Edvard Grieg's musical talents came from his Norwegian mother and not his Scottish father.

Their evidence is that she came from a "pure peasant family" and that she was the one who guided him on his musical way. Well, his father Alexander Grieg, the British Consul in Bergen, may not have told the world about the music in his soul but I'm sure it was there.

Gavin Greig's outstanding gifts were evidence that there was music in that side of the family.

My grandmother does not claim much knowledge of classical music but she knows a good rendering of Grieg's Piano Concerto when she hears it.

And last night in Aberdeen she was able to meet concert soloist Sheila Lessells, conductor Andrew Thomson and the others to tell them so.

LESTER PEARSON LOOKS AHEAD

—————— *15th September 1967* ——————

DATELINE: OTTOWA

He swivelled in his big leather chair and drank coffee from a saucerless cup. His pin-striped appearance was that of the local solicitor weighing up a client's case.

But the scene was Ottawa's Parliament Hill and the man was Lester Bowles Pearson, 14th Prime Minister of Canada, variously regarded as informal, friendly, complicated, and a master of dignified protocol.

The year has not been without its milestones for the former history professor who used to play third base for the Guelph Maple Leafs.

It brought not only the Centenary of Confederation for Canada but a 70th birthday for Mr Pearson—and he talked about the future of both, as well as of the problems confronting his great nation.

As we sat in the Premier's private room in the east wing I took my cue from Russia's Jacob Malik, who once said: "I always listen when Lester Pearson speaks."

"I think it is true that we have only now come of age as a nation," said Mr Pearson. "In the early part of our confederation history we were living in the shadow of

Downing Street Foreign policy. Defence policy and so on were determined in London.

"When we began to look after our own affairs, another shadow—not in any unfriendly sense—crossed the border from the south and we fell under the powerful economic and financial influence of the United States.

"Our way of life became North American and, in some ways, quite indistinguishable from the United States, except in Quebec. Now we realise in this centennial that it is a great thing to be a Canadian.

"It has given us a kind of pride and confidence in our identity and that has come to a head this year. We learned for the first time how to celebrate Canadianism with a kind of nationalistic fervour.

"One of the reasons why we have suspected patriotic breast-beating in the past may have been that the Scottish element is so strong.

"By tradition, the Scots don't go in for that. Their emotions run deep and do not readily show. So we were more reserved and there was a stability and dignity of life. But this has changed and I believe it is for the better.

"It helps to bring us together and, goodness knows, the creation of a strong national feeling in a country of this size is quite a problem.

"I welcome the outpouring. In fact I am becoming a Chauvinist myself!"

The issue of the moment in Canada is, of course, that of the two nations—English-speaking and French-speaking. Nearly half the Prime Minister's support is in the French-speaking province of Quebec, and many Canadians I spoke to were not only incensed by de Gaulle's recent "Vive le Quebec Libre!" speech but were also critical of Mr Pearson for allegedly pandering to the province.

This is what he had to say on the subject: "We are having

our problems with the relations of the two founding peoples, but I am confident no matter what the pessimists may say, that we will work it out—and work it out within a few years."

They would do so, he indicated, on a basis which would give the French-speaking people the feeling that they were real partners in Canadian development and that they have every opportunity inside Canada of maintaining unimpaired their own language, culture and tradition.

"We are making progress," he emphasised, "no matter what you may hear. The English-speaking part of the country is more aware than ever of the necessity of the dual foundation."

The Premier drank from his coffee cup, looked out towards the Mounties parading before Parliament Buildings, and talked of his country's emerging role of mediator.

Canada has been credited with a kind of balancing role between the United States and Britain and because of her special contacts with both had been able to interpret the point of view of each to the other.

It was a role which she could still play, he said, but its importance was sometimes exaggerated. The part Canada could play in situations such as the Middle East crisis was the kind of diplomacy which came mainly from direct contact with the U.S. and Britain.

The Commonwealth provided another big opportunity for external activity and Mr Pearson believed that its unique position as a multiracial association meant that it was more important than ever to keep it together.

Many immigrants to whom I spoke had clearly not found the streets of Canada paved with gold. So what of future population targets?

"We need a lot more people," said Mr Pearson, "but it is not so simple as it was in the early days when you could give a man a shovel and some grain and say: 'Go, dig yourself a livelihood.'

"You cannot settle a country that way now. You must integrate the new settlers into the economic structure and treat them as social security people from the beginning.

"We have been bringing in 250,000 people a year—that is as many as we can absorb and at that rate it will not take long to put the population up to 30 or 40 million.

"We are pushing the area of settlement further north all the time but there will be a proportion of Canada which will never have many people."

From the future of his country to more personal matters. And here Prime Minister Pearson may have given some hint of what lies ahead.

"I have been in public life since 1928. Before that I had begun in the academic field and I would like to finish there, too. One looks forward to an easier life and I cannot image any life which would not be easier than the one I live now.

"However, things are going well. I am feeling fine. And like Mr Diefenbaker, I make no predictions!"

There was a tap at the door. The Finance Minister was waiting. And the Italian President was coming too. Mr Pearson was apologetic for the hustle.

Another busy day was beginning in the Canadian capital. The work of a nation awaited.

THE COUNTRY BOY
FROM CUNNYKNOWE

———————— *16th September 1967* ————————

DATELINE: NEW YORK

Today in New York the top financiers of Wall Street, with America's Vice-President Hubert H. Humphrey as chief guest, will gather to pay tribute to the memory of a boy from an Aberdeenshire cottage called The Cunnyknowe.

And I will be there too—because it was my great-grandfather who helped set "the great humaniser of American business" on the road to fame and fortune.

The occasion is the 50th anniversary of the powerful business journal *Forbes Magazine* which has its base on Fifth Avenue, a few blocks from the Empire State Building.

It is a far cry from The Cunnyknowe, near Whitehill, in the parish of New Deer, where it all began.

The occupant at the tail-end of last century was Robbie Forbes, a tailor who struggled with rural poverty to bring up ten children, the sixth of which was little Bertie Charles Forbes, alert, intelligent and cheeky-faced.

Daily the youngsters trod the country road to Whitehill School, where they were well grounded in the reading, writing and 'rithmetic which formed the basis of a sound Scottish education. The dominie was my great-grandfather,

Gavin Greig.

When Dauvit Scott of the *Peterhead Sentinal* was looking for a printer's devil, he asked my great-grandfather to announce it in the class.

Bertie Forbes, soon to be 14, snapped his fingers in eager response. At a few shillings a week it was not much of a job, but it was a connection with writing, however slender, and that had become his interest.

He had learned the value of a bawbee by cleaning shoes and polishing silver at a nearby mansion. Now he was ready for the wider world.

From Peterhead he gained a foothold in journalism, and when the Boer War advertised the existence of South Africa, he set out for far horizons.

In Johannesburg, the great mystery writer Edgar Wallace was about to launch the *Rand Daily Mail*. He was immediately impressed by the young Scot who had gone out on to the golf courses there to caddie for the big business men, and learn from the conversation about an area of activity which fascinated him. The two men teamed up on the new paper, but another city beckoned for Forbes. By 1904, at the age of 24, he was off to New York.

There his modest reputation counted for nothing. A Scottish country-bumpkin—for that was how they regarded him—was unlikely material for the lofty world of finance, and he was politely told where to take himself.

That was until he offered to work for nothing. The *New York Journal of Commerce* admitted him to its humblest post. In next to no time B. C. Forbes was its respected financial editor.

At no time did he forget his native land. Every two years he came back; he endowed his local school and church, and entertained the parish folk to a gigantic picnic which was talked about until the next one.

In my own cub days in journalism, I watched him stand, on his 70th birthday, as the minister dedicated his latest gift to New Deer Church—a magnificent baptismal font.

Tears ran down his cheeks as a child from his own corner of the world was christened.

I remember listening open-mouthed as he told me how the famous newspaper-owning William Randolph Hearst once gave him a blank cheque to sign his own salary.

In 1917 he decided to capitalise on his name by starting his own business journal, *Forbes Magazine.*

In it, he pulled no punches. He was dedicated to big business but his days amid the farm servants of Aberdeenshire had ingrained in him that the worker must be rewarded.

In 1927 he conducted a searching campaign against Henry Ford entitled "Slave Driving in Ford Factories". Sometimes he lost advertising, but he kept his self-respect.

He was the close acquaintance of men like Andrew Carnegie, John D. Rockefeller and Frank Woolworth. He, too, became a millionaire, though he shirked the term.

At Christmas, 1953, Bertie Forbes made an unexpected visit to Scotland. He had a premonition that it was going to be his last, and, as in so many of his forecasts, he was right. The parish turned out to greet him and to watch as he disappeared over the hill on his last journey to America.

I am glad to have followed his path this day to be present at the celebration, for he was one of the first to encourage me in journalism.

Tonight I shall rise with the Vice-President of the United States, with Bertie's successor, his son Malcolm Forbes, and the men who run the great corporations of America to raise a cheer in memory of the lad from The Cunnyknowe.

His adopted land was the scene of his triumphs. But it will be appropriate if a faint echo of that cheer should reach that quiet corner of Scotland.

"The Sound of Music" ended its run at the Gaumont Cinema, Glasgow, on Saturday night after 1,723 performances seen by 1,564,928 people in a fantastic two-year and nine-month run.

WHEN LIFE ROLLS ALONG
ON THE SOUND OF MUSIC

———————— *25th December 1967* ————————

DATELINE: NEW YORK

I took a lift to the fourth floor of an office block in Madison Avenue, New York, and was shown into a well-appointed suite, hung with framed mementos.

It was a typical business suite in midtown Manhattan except, perhaps, for the modern paintings on the walls—and the grand piano in the corner.

The muted noise of traffic rising from the street was the nearest thing to the sound of music which I could hear as I settled down to talk to the legendary figure at the other side of the desk.

It was the small, dapper figure of Richard Rodgers, composer of as great a wealth of popular melodies as one man has ever produced.

It is hard to fit someone so unassuming into the legend—the memorable pre-war partnership of Rodgers and Hart, and then, on the death of Lorenz Hart, the greater partnership of Rodgers and Hammerstein.

That second period alone had given the world musical plays which ranged from *Oklahoma* and *Carousel* to *South Pacific*, *The King and I* and *The Sound of Music*.

Richard Rodgers looks a business man and adds to the picture by travelling to his office most days, either from his home in Manhattan or in Fairfield, Connecticut.

"I am not the kind of composer who wakes up in the middle of the night with an idea and springs out of bed to put it down on paper," he says. "I have to sit down and concentrate—and work.

"It begins with the idea of the play, the situation and the character. If I have a lyric I can go ahead and write the music. Sometimes I do the music first. But the important thing is the situation and the character. And that is usually provided by someone else . . ."

The "someone else" who inspired the melodic genius of Rodgers to reach its heights was, respectively, Lorenz Hart and Oscar Hammerstein II, the men who wrote the words.

Both are now dead. Since Hammerstein went, in 1960, Rodgers has written *No Strings* which was a success in America, and *Do I Hear a Waltz*, which failed.

Richard Rodgers, at 65, has not found a satisfactory third partner. But he has accumulated a massive fortune, which has not been lessened by the proceeds from *The Sound of Music*. While well aware of its success, he was astounded to hear that it was still running in the same Glasgow cinema after two years and nine months.

"I haven't been to Britain for several years and I was last in Glasgow in 1930 for the opening of *Evergreen*. So *The Sound of Music* is still running there," he mused. "It is a film which has an enormous number of ingredients which are popular."

I touched on a delicate subject, on which Rodgers is prepared to talk briefly but rationally: Cancer.

"Yes, it is true I had cancer. I have not kept it a secret. It was in the jaw. But that was twelve years ago and I was cured. As a matter of fact, I had a check-up for it yesterday and I'm all right."

As we shook hands, I felt that I was leaving a lonesome man, a man who had taken us through a chorus of tunefulness from *Blue Moon* to that last song which he and Oscar Hammerstein sat down to write together—*Edelweiss*.

His consolation is that his music cheers. The winds which sweep down the plains of Oklahoma blow just as surely in the far corners of rural Scotland where many a farm lad or village message boy goes about his work whistling a happy tune with little thought for who wrote it.

Richard Rodgers told me: "I would like my music to live." And it will.

IT ALL STARTED ON
A SUNDAY AT CRIMOND

——————— *8th April 1968* ———————

A psalm was being sung at Crimond Church, Aberdeenshire, one Sunday in the mid-50's when a teenage boy made his racing debut, unknown to his parents, on the adjoining airfield.

That day the minister objected to the noise of the cars. Yesterday the roar of the young man, Jim Clark, stopped suddenly in Germany. [He was killed, aged 32, while practising at Hockenheim.]

Between times, Jim Clark had become not only the greatest racing driver in world history but an ambassador for his native Scotland such as she has seldom had before.

There was little of the tearaway extrovert that one might associate with a dare-devil sport like car-racing. The eyes, which would be steely blue-grey one moment, turned quickly to the crinkle of laughter. The hands of this son of a Border farmer were long and slender, with gently tapering fingers and immaculate nails—the hands of an artist or musician.

His voice had an international flavour, basically Scottish but with the nasal overtones of America and Australia.

Above all, his demeanour was that of a modest gentleman, conducting himself with good sense and good taste wherever he went.

It was Jim Clark of *Scotland*—a fact which he never forgot. For many people in distant corners of the world it was the first time they had even stopped to consider that such a country existed. It was their first impression—and it could not have been more favourable.

Back home, he would change into the role of farmer as he surveyed his acres near Duns. He was at ease as the sheep farmer, chatting to his neighbours, taking his animals to market.

His father farmed nearby, having moved from Kilmeny in Fife. Jim, who was educated at Loretto School in Edinburgh, was put in charge of a farm when he was a youth.

He also acquired a passion for fast cars. His parents did not know he was slipping away to race at weekends.

His mother once said: "I'll never forget the day I found out. He had been travelling regularly up to Crimond to act as mechanic for a friend who raced there.

"Then one day, when he was driving me over to his farm, he said: 'Mum, what would you say if I told you that I had been competing in the races?' What could I say? He was grown up by then."

Mrs Clark has four daughters. Jim was her only boy. When he was racing she would move away from the TV set.

Once she said: "I know Jim is very level-headed and wouldn't take risks. He would miss all the friends he has made through racing and travel. But I'll be happy the day he gives it up."

How sad that Jim Clark should have left us so soon.

The consolation—if there is one—is simply that, if the likelihood of death had not been there, his particular opportunity for positive living and example would not have been there either.

WHAT THE ARCHITECT NOTICED
ABOUT KNIVES AND FORKS

———————— *16th August 1968* ————————

His name was Charles Rennie Mackintosh, a Glasgow architect who raised plenty of controversy in his day. He designed fine buildings, found himself the high success of an international reputation and then, all too soon, melted away to the wilderness.

He drank too much and died of cancer in 1928. But what is more important is that, in a Scotland which has excelled at producing great architects, Mackintosh was as great as any.

And whatever neglect there has been in the past there is in this, his centenary year—and according to a familiar pattern—a great deal of fresh recognition.

A special exhibition is ready to open with the Edinburgh Festival this weekend. And today brings the publication of a new book by Robert Macleod, assistant director of the Institute of Advanced Architectural Studies at York University.

Charles Rennie Mackintosh was the son of a Glasgow policeman, one of 11 children who said all along that he was going to be an architect.

At 16 he was articled to the Glasgow firm of John

Hutchison but later joined Messrs Honeyman and Keppie (where he became a partner) and won a "Greek" Thomson scholarship which took him to Italy.

It was around the turn of the century that he reached his peak with what is commonly regarded as his masterpiece—the design of Glasgow's new School of Art.

Mackintosh emerged as the leading exponent of the Art Nouveau and the precursor of some of the most advanced trends in architecture.

In Glasgow he came to know Miss Catherine Cranston, who was establishing herself in a big way with that largely Glasgow phenomenon, the tea-room. He became closely identified with the decoration of Cranston premises.

Mackintosh concerned himself not only with the design of buildings but with the furnishings which would make the complete piece—down to the forks and knives.

He had the sense, for example, to see that we use only the last inch of a knife to cut our meat so he designed a knife with a short blade and long handle. Similarly he gave his fork only three short prongs, which was all that was necessary.

But there came a time, as with so many men of genius, when his affairs began to deteriorate. The working routine was becoming less and less bearable and he was antagonising clients and colleagues alike, according to Macleod's book.

He resigned in 1913, went to Suffolk, and then Chelsea and in 1923, to Port Vendres, in the south of France, where he devoted himself to water-colour painting. In 1927 he complained of a sore throat and returned to London where cancer of the tongue and throat was diagnosed. He died the following year.

WHO NEEDS 'BLUE' FILMS
TO TEACH SEX TO A CHILD?

─────────────── *19th August 1968* ───────────────

I have an eight-year-old son who is meanwhile enjoying his summer holidays on his grandfather's farm in Aberdeenshire. One of the daily pleasures is to look after his cow.

Oh yes, it is *his* cow. He took his total savings out of the bank in the spring and paid cash at the cattle mart for his black and white heifer.

He knows the difference between a cow and a bull and he will no doubt have the chance to acquaint himself with their relationship and to gain a working knowledge of the reproductive processes.

We have never burdened him with the cabbage leaf or gooseberry bush theories. He knows where he came from and is absorbing the basic facts of life in a perfectly simple and natural manner which has neither disturbed himself nor embarrassed his parents.

All of which seems a great deal more desirable than the continuing flood of adult frenzies which seek to dot the "i's" and cross the "t's" of a subject with which the vast majority of young people have a consuming familiarity.

When it comes to assessing the sexual knowledge of the young, the not-so-young are incredibly naive.

The latest fancy of a film strip company in England, I see, is to plan a film, for the digestion of school-children, showing a naked couple making love—to the accompaniment of a commentary by a disc jockey!

Work will begin, I understand, as soon as they find a suitable couple for the starring roles. Not that that should prove difficult. Couples are going at it every day for the blue film industry.

But the producers want a normal married couple of good moral character.

That will be harder to find. Because the exhibition they would be expected to give is a fundamentally private function whose naturalness would suffer defeat from the very presence of a camera crew, not to mention the knowledge of a vast, unseen audience.

It is just one more prize example of man's unfailing capacity for making an ass of himself.

Of course there should be sensible instruction for the young but let us not be carried away by our own enthusiasms. Many of the wide-eyed pleas of the young when they land in some bother that they "didn't know" are so much poppycock.

I well remember some of the earlier attempts at sex instruction in school when we boys and girls feigned monumental ignorance—to see how much the teacher knew! And that was not an isolated example.

It is not from any sense of shock that I advocate allowing our young people, who have a lot more sense than we permit, to absorb the subject of sex in a natural, seemly and healthy way.

Let them enjoy their childhood for as long as it will last—which is not very long—and let them gain their knowledge at a pace which is in keeping with their curiosity.

Let the film strip people keep their strip films for other

places.

I am much happier that my young son is learning from the surroundings of nature—from the cows and the bulls on the lush pasture lands of Aberdeenshire.

SO NEAR, THE FIREMAN'S
WORD FOR HORROR

—————————— *19th November 1968* ——————————

The firemen at James Watt Street yesterday had thoughts only for the job.

But if they had had time to look around, they might have remembered the place only a few hundred yards away, which will forever be a synonym for horror in the firemen's vocabulary: Cheapside.

It was there, on a Monday in March, 1960, that 19 of their colleagues died trying to quell a blaze in a whisky warehouse.

The building blew outwards, sending its masonry crashing on to the fire engines below.

A few hundred yards the other way is the site of the Grafton fashion store, in which 13 shop girls died on the afternoon of May 4, 1949.

But yesterday was a time for action, not memories.

The place where 20 died had three floors with a frontage of only nine windows.

The signboard said: "B. Stern (Upholstery) Ltd., established 1919. Suites and chairs re-covered."

Inside were the people who re-covered them, people who had gone to work as usual on a Monday morning not knowing the goodbyes they had taken—or had perhaps forgotten to take—would be their last.

Outside were the fire-fighters, the police and the helpless onlookers who could only stand and stare and reconstruct the horror of the anguished screams that came from within, as victims grappled with iron-barred windows in a last, despairing bid to live.

Gradually the scene built up. To a maze of hoses and foam, tenders and firemen perched on high ladders was added the blue-flash of ambulances whose emptiness was, for once, a bad sign.

As word spread, relatives began to arrive at the mobile police headquarters seeking news, poised between hope and apprehension.

There was the woman whose husband was said to have been out for a cup of coffee at the time. If that were so, where was he?

Accompanied by a seamen's mission chaplain she searched local cafes but returned without hope.

The crowd respectfully made avenues for those who hurried towards the police van, praying against their worst fears, only to emerge in a state of collapse.

On derelict property nearby, some tatty, out-of-date posters called for aid to Vietnam.

But there was an emergency nearer home. They were people in that building over there who had needed help.

People whose screams had gone silent on a dull Glasgow morning and for whom there was nothing more to be done.

The phrase "kinky sex" entered the vocabulary of North-east Scotland in 1968 as the result of a murder trial in Aberdeen. The on-goings of well-to-do Mearns farmer Max Garvie, his wife Sheila and their respective lovers made a sordid tale which ended in Garvie's disappearance. When I visited his farm at the end of the trial I heard his neighbours' reaction.

MAXWELL GARVIE

The Other Side of the Man
Whose Name Shook the World!

―――――――――― *13th December 1968* ――――――――――

Bill Scorgie, the solid farm grieve on whom Max Garvie depended for the running of West Cairnbeg, talked yesterday about the master who disappeared in the night—to become the subject of Scotland's most dramatic-ever murder story.

He broke through his natural reticence the day after local reaction to the sensational trial boiled up to an effusion of sympathy for the dead man and an eagerness to show that the Max Garvie they knew as neighbour and friend was a vastly different person from the image of a monster which emerged at the trial.

Garvie's wife, Sheila, and her lover Brian Tevendale, began life sentences for his murder last week.

Mr Scorgie, who was among the signatories to a statement which appeared in yesterday's *Scottish Daily Express*, talked quietly in his cottage just 100 yards from the big farmhouse in which Max Garvie was shot.

He was the witness who was not called at the trial, the man who drove Mrs Garvie's mother to the police at the beginning of the whole investigation.

He said: "I was in close touch with Max and always found him a good employer. He had time to stop and have a word with the farmworkers but with Mrs Garvie it was different. She would drive down the road there, with her black specs on and her nose in the air.

"She would talk panloaf sometimes and then fall down through it, whereas Max spoke to us in a local way.

"Whenever he was going anywhere he would always tell me; that was why I began to think something had happened when there was no word from him. It was not like Max to do a thing like that.

"As for Mrs Garvie, the thing that sticks with me, is that she told me all those lies after it happened. Yes, yes, it's the lies . . .

"When Max was here he attended to his business. There was no question of him being the fast-living chap who neglected things. He left me to get on with organising the farmwork and he attended to the office work and was there to help with the harvest, or the potatoes, or things like that.

"We were not involved in his social life, so we knew nothing of the parties. But in the past year, he did begin to get careless. I knew he was worried about his wife and the fact that he was losing her."

Mr Scorgie was among the group of local people who had gathered at the neighbouring farm of Auchcairnie where Mr Douglas Argo played host to the group of local people who issued the statement in support of Max Garvie's character.

Their words and action were a true reflection of the widespread desire in the district to rectify what they believe to be a totally false impression of the man.

It was not so much a bid to whitewash Garvie, but to show that the side which they knew was something totally different.

Most people concede that there must have been a side to his character that they did not know. It is merely a surprise to them that it did not show through at some stage in their experience.

A local veterinary surgeon said: "Any time I was up at West Cairnbeg testing cattle, he would be up there in the morning ready and willing and fit to help.

"He might have been a bit harum scarum but you got the impression from the trial that he was probably a loud, vulgar, objectionable man and in fact he was none of these things.

"He was a pleasant, fairly modest, intelligent man."

One of the people in regular contact with Max Garvie—he called at West Cairnbeg only a few hours before the murder—was the well known North East entertainer and broadcaster Mr John Mearns, who works as an agricultural representative in the Kincardineshire area.

He said: "We had the contract to supply feeding stuff for Max's 1,400 pigs and I used to call on him every Tuesday. He was an outstanding personality and I can honestly say that in all 40 years in this job there was never a customer whom I respected more highly.

"Shortly before all this happened I remember calling on him as usual and he said 'come away John you are just in time for coffee' and Mrs Garvie brought in the tray and wee Lloyd was there. I just thought to myself what a happy family picture it was, making nonsense of the rumours that Mrs Garvie had been away from him.

"Max kept his office well laid out with a record of his pigs; he pioneered the growing of carrots as well as a new potato planting machine. He would talk flying. He was keen to encourage people to fly and was always going to take me up some time. I asked him if he thought planes were going to replace motor cars in the Mearns, but he didn't think that would come about."

On the afternoon of May 14—hours before the murder

took place upstairs—John Mearns made his regular call.

"It was a lovely afternoon and when I got there Mrs Garvie was working in the greenhouse with the little boy beside her—a happy picture. She had asked me to bring a sample of dog nuts and little Lloyd fed them to the dog.

"She apologised that Max wasn't at home and I arranged to phone the following morning."

John Mearns did phone but Mrs Garvie was never to be there again.

Said Mr A. J. Milne from Lawsondale Cottage, Kingswells, Aberdeen: "I am not surprised that the local people are incensed at the character attributed to Max Garvie. He spent most of his weekends at the flying club at Fordoun, along with ordinary, everyday folk from all walks of life who found him a most fair and considerate person.

"My two daughters are about the age of Max's daughters and have often flown with him. They were treated exactly as a normal father would treat his children and they had every respect for him."

A neighbouring farmer, Mr Harry Lindsay said: "I knew him mainly in connection with the Auchenblae Farmers Ball. He wisnae the kind o' lad who got fu' at dances and was aggressive like some folks you see. He was never coarse or used bad language, especially if there were women about. I just knew him as an obliging kind o' man."

At the Marine Hotel, on Stonehaven's harbour front— the venue of the district's alleged "jet set"—Mrs Jean Robertson, the proprietor's wife said: "If they brought a petition about Maxwell Garvie's character down here, there would be a rush of signatures. To those who knew him, there was that terribly helpless feeling as they read how much a monster he was painted in court.

"We *knew* he wasn't like that. Homosexual? Never. A monster? What cruel, utter nonsense."

In the hotel where the Garvies were said to have openly cavorted, there was no one to speak ill of the man. Instead, there was a frank estimate—Maxwell was Maxwell. There was astonishment at any suggestion that he wasn't a normal, likeable man, of some dignity.

And so it went on. Meanwhile, the farmhouse at West Cairnbeg stood quiet in its attractive grounds on a dead December day. The children's home-made swing, once a symbol of happiness, hung limp on the spacious lawn.

The scene of the murder seemed all too peaceful in this serene setting of the Mearns where the peewits swoop and the fine red soil falls away into the sea by Bervie and Gourdon.

Bill Scorgie finished his dinner and went out to direct his nine men to their afternoon's work.

At West Cairnbeg, the work had to go on as usual.

ON BERLIN PATROL
—WITH THE ARGYLLS!

At Dawn, with the Border Guards, the East-West
Situation Comes Alive at a Glance

————————— *22nd May 1969* —————————

DATELINE: BERLIN

Here, in the Divided City, split across by a wall and an entanglement of barbed wire, those rugged Scots from Paisley, Dumbarton, Argyllshire or Stirling have come to guard the border area, to flex the muscles of Western democracy and to boost the morale of the West Berliner encased in his cocoon of poignant drama.

On all sides lie the Communist lands of East Germany except for the narrow access corridor through which our plane flew low and guardedly to touch down at Gatow Airport, former Luftwaffe base.

You don't have far to travel to find the 700 glengarried men. Their new home is a beautiful estate which was once the quarters of the Luftwaffe but now carries the more appropriate name of Montgomery Barracks.

It sits hard by the barbed wire barricades of East Germany, about 12 miles out from the Brandenburg Gate, with Communist sentries gazing intently over the camp from their lofty watch-towers.

Goering had a house just outside the gate. Hitler used to bring Eva Braun up to the Haus Carow, a country pub along the road, for a weekend meal.

But now the principal actors have gone, leaving a ghostly memory which is largely condemned by the younger Berliner, quietly revered, one suspects, by many of his elders, and which follows the visitor wherever he goes.

The Argyll gets on with his duty regardless, based in his Scottish community of soldiers, wives and children, Army clubs, Naafi shops and barracks school, all set among wooded grounds and spacious sports fields.

High poplars line the route out of Montgomery Barracks and it was through this sylvan guard of honour that I drove one morning last week, seated uncomfortably in the back of an Army vehicle, en route for the dawn patrol of the border between West Berlin and East Germany.

In charge of this six-man reconnaissance patrol was Lieut. Hamish Clark (24) an exiled Scot from the Isle of Wight. With him were Corporal Alex Muir (26) from Paisley, Corporal Hugh Haggarty (28), from Bargeddie, and Privates Peter Ralston (21), Cumbernauld, Eddie Wilson (19), Greenock and Jim Hunter (20), Falkirk.

We drove to the north-west corner of the British sector and mounted the first vantage point to see what was happening on the other side of the fence. The fence, alas, is no longer just a barbed wire.

For the Russians are in the process of building a concrete wall right round West Berlin to match the one which already cuts the city in two.

Lieutenant Clark immediately grabbed binoculars. Something unusual seemed to be happening. A platoon of East German soldiers, more than usual, was being marched up for duty. Two officers in charge, as well as two armed guards. Odd. Normally N.C.O.s take this responsibility. Why officers?

Corporal Muir rests his binoculars on his barricades and

trains them on the party. He reports the ranks of the men and what they are doing. Lieutenant Clark makes careful note. It will all be logged, yesterday, today and all the tomorrows and whatever mysteries obtain for the moment there will eventually emerge a pattern which will make some kind of sense to the Intelligence services.

This morning's duties for the East German soldiers include the raking of long beds of sand which stretch well back from the boundary walls and whose function is to record the footsteps of would-be defectors.

But the barbed wire and the walls are not all that make an escape from East Germany a hazardous task. There are booby traps, guard dogs and sentries galore—tough, ruthless men—ready to shoot on sight for the bonus payment it brings them.

Across the sentry tower, two East German guards train their binoculars back on us. The fact that there are two strangers in the Argyll party, including photographer Peter MacVean with an array of camera equipment, means that there is something special to be logged on the other side.

In the grey mists of early morning, the whole story of the Berlin situation comes alive almost at a glance. We move down the border in our two-vehicle patrol and stop frequently to scale a tree or climb a watchtower.

Every movement over the Wall goes down on record. A bunch of young soldiers are putting up a new sentry post. Another squad seem to be laying a new wiring system. Is it a trip-wire or a communication line? They pause and gaze over at the Argylls.

The British soldier has instructions not to make the conversation but to respond politely to any courtesy. This particular lot of East Germans have a sense of humour.

They are well within shouting distance and they call to Corporal Muir: "Why don't you come on this side? It's better over here." He replies with a similar invitation.

Another call, to Corporal Haggarty, is more loaded. "How long are you here for?" asks the East German. Haggarty has the sense not to reply.

Here and there we pause at a little cross, marking the spot where some poor unfortunate has been shot dead in the bid for freedom. It is the story of Berlin.

We left the Border Patrol and drove down the main processional route of Berlin, from the Heerstrasse down the Kaiserdamm and Bismarckstrasse to the Brandenburg Gate. If it were not for the notorious Wall, you could drive straight through to the Unter den Linden to complete what must be one of the most impressive sweeps of city roadway in the world.

At several points along the Wall there are spectator platforms where the West Berliner takes his family on a Sunday to wave across to relatives on the other side.

We drove up past the Olympic Stadium and the adjoining Maifeld sports ground where Hitler made so many of those hysterical speeches one sees on old newsreels.

But all is silent now, except for the ra-ta-tat of gunfire on the neighbouring military combat area, where I found the Argylls going through a rigorous training session of street fighting and house-to-house clearance.

There they were, tough, agile Scottish soldiers darting from house to house dealing swiftly and efficiently with a situation which could conceivably arise right there in West Berlin. Amid deafening gunfire, company commander Major Alastair Scott-Elliott from Dumfries watched as Lieutenant Malcolm McVittie put his men through their paces.

Ben Douglas, square-cut sergeant from Earlston, bawled instructions as the first prisoner was marched out of the firing line. The "prisoner" was 19-year-old George Murray from Dumbarton, being covered by the gun of Private Ernest

Whyte (24) from Rutherglen. Whyte has seen the real thing in Aden. Now it was practice but hardly less intense.

We drew away from the Argylls in action and drove quietly past another spot where very soon they will be in action.

It is Spandau Jail, a simple red-brick building made to hold 600 prisoners but currently the captivity of only one man, Hitler's former deputy, Rudolf Hess.

By the end of May it will be the turn of the Argylls to stand guard over the ageing, pathetic figure who came on a would-be peace mission one morning in 1941 and landed by parachute at Floors Farm, Eaglesham, on the outskirts of Glasgow.

From their watch-towers, these Scottish soldiers will be able to see Rudolf Hess exercising in the prison yard.

At the gates of Spandau one gets an urge to go inside and have a look at this remnant of a force which changed the whole face of history.

Since that is not possible, I drove back instead along the boundary wall and through the guard post of Montgomery Barracks, contemplating the madness of it all and ready to enjoy an evening meal in the baronial splendour of the Officers' Mess.

WHEN THE TAX ON RUM
WAS A FARTHING A GALLON!

—————————— *31st July 1969* ——————————

Thomas Walter Donald nods towards a portrait above his lounge mantel-piece and tells you that the robust gentleman in question, his great-great-grandfather, was born in 1745 and became one of Glasgow's tobacco lords trading with the American colonies.

But Mr Donald, quiet and cultured, does not require a portrait to give his visitor a sense of history.

For he himself has lived through 92 years in which he has been, and remains, an active city lawyer.

He was a trustee of the estate of Mr Smith of Blythswood Square, father of Madeleine Smith, the Glasgow girl accused in 1857 of poisoning her secret French lover, a charge which was found "not proven".

The other day Mr Donald brought another reminder of an age that is all but forgotten when he called a rather special meeting of the Glasgow West India Association.

The association was founded in 1807 to help those eager businessmen who were trading with the West Indies during last century to bring home the rum, sugar and tobacco.

"My family has turned from trading to law, however," says Mr Donald, "and I was never a trader myself. I merely became treasurer of the West India Association in the 1930's, by which time there was not much business being done.

"The emancipation of the slaves had knocked a considerable hole in the profits.

"But there was a time in the heyday of these tobacco, rum and sugar lords when the association was very active. In 1840, for example, it appointed a delegation to go to Parliament to protest against an increase in the duty of rum from a farthing to a halfpenny per gallon.

"Glasgow was doing a tremendous overseas trade at that time. By the time the Second World War came, more and more trade was being done from London.

"Those in Glasgow still interested began to die off and the association became moribund. We met again in 1946—but not again until 1969, when I thought it was perhaps about time we had another meeting."

This time is was to see about disposing of stock and cash totalling around £730—and eight remaining members of a once-flourishing organisation agreed that the remaining surplus funds will be handed over to "the West India Committee", London.

This is a non-profit making body, founded in 1750, which promotes Commonwealth, Caribbean/U.K. trade and stimulates investment in the Commonwealth and Caribbean and the improvement of the standard of living there.

In his luxury flat in Glasgow's west end, Mr Donald showed me the massive tomes of minutes stretching back to 1807, which are now being handed over to the Mitchell Library. He has known nearly half of that period from his own experience.

To talk to him was to absorb history itself. At 92, he is still senior partner in one of Scotland's biggest legal practices. He pops down to the Western Club in the city centre, or off on a cruise to Madeira.

WHEN A TOWN LIVES—AND DIES—BY THE SEA

———————— 22nd January 1970 ————————

DATELINE: FRASERBURGH

They mourn quietly in this Aberdeenshire fishing town tonight, for demonstration is not in their nature. They live by the sea, which gives them their daily bread. And they are prepared to die by the sea, like the five lifeboatmen who perished today.

They never pause to question their fate, these people whose faith and courage mark them out in the category of very special human beings.

I am standing tonight on the foreshore at Fraserburgh, on the very spot where I stood one winter's day just 17 years ago.

Around me then stood a vast crowd of local fisher folk, urging and applauding a powerful swimmer whom they knew as Andrew Ritchie.

"Come on Andra," they shouted, "Come on man, come on man, ye'll make it," as if the prize might be an Olympic medal.

The prize was even greater.

For the previous Fraserburgh lifeboat, the *John and Charles Kennedy*, had just turned turtle at the mouth of the harbour on a clear, sunlit but turbulent day, within shouting distance of the crewmen's firesides.

Five men died then, trapped under their craft as they frantically struggled to swim under and out.

Coxswain Andrew Ritchie had managed to escape and, with what strength was left in his battered body, he was reaching out for his wife and children, no more than 100 yards to go, as the crowd roared helplessly across an angry sea.

His prize was life—and he lost it, when he was struck by a piece of floating wreckage.

Fraserburgh had lost its lifeboat, as it had done a generation before and it has done again today.

On that night in 1953, I sat with old Mrs Tait, whose husband had died in the disaster and whose son Charlie was the sole survivor, and marvelled at her philosophy in an hour of grief.

"Better," she said quietly, "that young Charles should live, for he has young bairns to look after."

And so it is with the fisher folk of Scotland.

When they called a meeting on the following week to recruit a new crew, Andrew Ritchie's brother came forward to offer himself as coxswain. Charlie Tait came back and brought his brother to fill their father's place.

Old Robert Scott, the lifeboat's secretary, wept in his gratitude.

For the men who go down to the sea in little ships do not stop to count the cost.

The lifeboat duty is a mission of mercy which they themselves, as fishermen, may need tomorrow.

So they go to help save the lives of men from home and foreign ports who would do the same for them.

Just as they went today and all their yesterdays.

Just as they went in 1940 when they sailed away from

Fraserburgh and Peterhead with their small fishing boats to rescue men from the beaches at Dunkirk.

And just as, for certain, their successors will go at the first calling of a new boat.

It is the way of things in a town like Fraserburgh.

Away to my left the Kinnaird Head Lighthouse flashes its hypnotic beam, cool and eerie.

To the right lies the magnificent sandy stretch of the town's famous holiday beach.

Behind is the town itself with its Saltoun Square and Dalrymple Hall, its neat streets and fine people.

There is a wailing in the wind outby tonight.

And a quiet prayer in the homes and hearts of people who are not ashamed to tell you where they find their hope and inspiration and comfort.

I'M ON MY WAY TO HAMPDEN
. . . ON A CHARIOT!

—————————— *9th February 1970* ——————————

At the final whistle on Saturday afternoon I danced a little jig of joy and left a football ground with a headful of dreams about the final at Hampden Park in May.

No, I wasn't at Celtic Park or Forfar, or anywhere else in the upper echelons of the Soccer scene. I was at Minishant, in Ayrshire, a hamlet with an undisputed claim to the worst-ever football pitch in Christendom. But Minishant are leading lights in amateur circles, having been recent winners of the Scottish Amateur Cup. Visiting teams are at an immediate disadvantage in that they usually come untrained for hill walking and treading upon corrugated sod.

But whatever took me to Minishant on Saturday? It is a story which goes back to my boyhood in the village of Maud in Aberdeenshire, more than 20 years ago.

We hadn't much by way of amusement but we did have a football team and when they had exhausted all the reserve power, they would on occasion call upon me to play. For I was, and remain, an enthusiast.

You could depend on the Webster Wiggle to mesmerise 'em some. My double shuffle astonished all, especially myself, and I was always good for a laugh if nothing else.

106

And in those far off times, I dreamed that one day Maud might play at the famous Hampden Park.

I would waken in the middle of the night in a cold sweat, having run the full length of the sacred turf, beating all comers to score the winner and be chaired round the track by delirious team-mates.

All romantic nonsense, of course. But was it?

A generation later my little village of Maud still has its football team. In the current season they decided to come out of the garden and try their luck among the 320 teams in the Scottish Amateur Cup. There was nothing to lose.

They survived the first round and the second, the third and then the fourth, and on Saturday they tackled the 480-mile round trip to Minishant for the fifth round.

The village came by the bus load, though the population is only 800. The few exiles like myself augmented the ranks, and there we stood by the village pitch at Minishant out-numbering the locals by about 2-1 and shouting our vociferous support in the broad dialect of the North-East.

The main road passed down one touchline, balls had to be retrieved from the burn down the other. Sleet came and went but I remained lost in my enthusiasm. This was football as it should be played and enjoyed and if I could no longer give Maud the benefit of the famous Wiggle, I would give them my heart and voice, playing out every move with the man on the ball.

Maud went two up, but Minishant pulled one back and it was exciting touch-and-go stuff till the very last gasp. Imagine the spectacle of relief when the final whistle blew and I ran on to the pitch waving my golf umbrella in sheer ecstasy. Maybe all men really are boys at heart.

In any case, Maud were through to the last 16 in the Scottish Amateur Cup. They are undefeated in 50 league games, and just three more wins in the Cup would take them to that Hampden final.

Dare I anticipate that impossible dream of yesteryear will come true on May 9? If so, I'll promise to ride to Hampden Park in a chariot. And buy the champagne, of course.

PS: Maud failed to reach Hampden, but only at the last hurdle.

THE MAN WHO IS PUTTING
LAUGHTER ON SHOW

————————— *7th March 1970* ——————

> *Winter's came,*
> *The snow has fell,*
> *Wee Josis nosis frozis well;*
> *Wee Josis frozis nosis skintit;*
> *Winter's diabolic—intit?*

It is many moons since Scotland first saw a newspaper cartoon of the wee, cold bedraggled Glesca character standing at the bus stop, accompanied by the caption above.

There are many today who still recall it as a gem of Glasgow expression and the work of former West of Scotland bus driver, Bud Neill.

Since then his name has gained household proportions throughout the country with his cartoons in the *Scottish Daily Express*.

For Bud Neill is the versifier who began to put drawings to his pithy sayings by breaking all the accepted rules of art, creating what some people thought had neither proportion nor sense, and ending up with an overall effect which is widely acclaimed as genius.

Confirmation of his acceptance in all stratas comes today when the Scottish Arts Council honour him by opening a four-week exhibition at their galleries in Blythswood Square, Glasgow.

It contains not only a large selection of his small cartoons and larger format works, but such items as a coloured strip of the Battle of Bannockburn and cartoons created by cameraless photography.

But what kind of man is he, this controversial artist who delights so many, appals a few but scrapes on regardless, in his own highly original way?

If you can accept in one sentence that he has been a soldier, a funeral undertaker and a bus driver, that he lives in a Post Office instead of a house and drives a van instead of a car, you get some idea that he is not the kind of chap you can readily pigeon-hole.

The converted Post Office at Halbeath, in Fife, is the retreat where he leads a life that smacks of the recluse. There he reads his morning papers, gets the feel of the day's news, sits down with pen and ink to produce a topical laugh and put it on the train for the *Express* office in Glasgow—all before 11am!

Yet the figure of the man has nothing to do with long hair and arty-crafty gestures. What hair he has he combs forward.

Bud Neill is approaching his 60th year ("I came off the assembly line the year before the Model T Ford"), having been born in the Partick district of Glasgow and reared in Troon, where his father was in the chemical business.

By his own insistence, he was nobody's academic dream, Bud the Dud, in fact, if you take his word for it.

"I wasn't bad at drawing and quite good at English because I was interested," he explains. "But I was singularly stupid at figures."

They were in two minds about taking him into art school in Glasgow but they relented and he went for a commercial course.

"When I was discharged from the Army during the war the only thing I could do was drive, so I got a job on Alexanders' buses, first from the Milngavie depot then driving between Glasgow and Neilston.

"One day I was on the tea break in Clyde Street, Glasgow, gnawing away at my cheese piece, when I read a letter to an editor deploring the habits of Glasgow bus drivers. I replied in defence and apparently my pungency took the attention of newspaper editors.

"Verses had always been with me. They're like fleas—you just can't get rid of them."

It was then only a matter of teaming up his verbal wit with his wildly unconventional drawings to produce the cartoons which have gained such a large audience.

Bud Neill says he is never short of an idea and prefers to think of himself more as a commentator than a cartoonist.

Although happily married, Bud Neill is essentially a lonesome man, a rugged individualist. He once had a horror of his three sons becoming bankers or accountants, so he looked around for something likely and lucrative—and sent them all to be waiters!

All three are now carving promising careers for themselves in the hotel trade.

The only thing that troubles Bud is his memory. With ridiculous accuracy, he can tell you that he gave up drinking on May 7, 1960. The rest is not so easy.

"I'm suffering from some kind of aberration of the . . . they're worried about it, you know . . . aberration of the . . .

"My memory is diabolic—intit?"

THOSE BBC ACCENTS WOULD BE
THE 'SPEAK' OF THE MEARNS!

29th March 1970

That great masterpiece of the Scottish soil, *Sunset Song*, has finally reached our television screens in the form of a BBC2 serial which will be seen throughout Britain every Friday for the next five weeks.

For thousands of Scots, let alone the other assorted inhabitants of these islands, it is a first meeting with the works of Lewis Grassic Gibbon, a modern Scottish author whose name already appears on school examination papers along with Scott and Stevenson.

Gibbon—real name James Leslie Mitchell—was born at Auchterless, Aberdeenshire in 1901, grew up at Arbuthnott, in the Mearns, and was dead before his 34th birthday.

His folk were crofters who little understood his genius and in that they were hardly to be blamed, for such spirits are often a trial to honest, hard-working people!

But Leslie Mitchell knew his purpose. And his gift for absorbing the sounds and sights and rhythms of the Scottish countryside, its grey drudgery and warm humanity, and reproducing them in peerless prose, fully justified his deviation from the tradition of following his father on the land. It was a grudging land and a grudging father.

112

Chris Guthrie was to become his central character in three novels, the first of which was *Sunset Song*, published in 1932.

And what about the opening episode of the £50,000 television series? Inevitably, it is a time for character-drawing, and in the limited time I believe the BBC did not do too badly with a novel which was written to be read. But I had reservations.

Having fallen in love with Chris all of 20 years ago, I found her disappointing when taken away from my imagination. Nor was Long Rob of the Mill anywhere near my impression of Rob's appearance and power, though I am assured he emerges strongly as time goes on.

I found the accents a rather illegitimate mixture of Glasgow Highland and pseudo-English instead of Lowland, to which part the North-East of Scotland undoubtedly belongs.

I wonder why the BBC must always apologise for the North-East accent? In travels around the world I have always found that my Aberdeenshire tongue is counted among my greater assets.

Chae Strachan came across as the most truly authentic accent, which is explained by actor Victor Carin's own links with the area.

My other complaint was with a distracting flicker which, I understand, was due to a technical flaw.

Yesterday I talked to Grassic Gibbon's widow, 69 year-old Mrs Ray Mitchell, a retired Treasury official who still lives in Welwyn Garden City, where her husband died in 1935. How did it go down with her English neighbours, I wondered.

"Very well," she replied. "Except that they didn't understand words like 'thole'. Two other points baffled them— and I agree that they were not made sufficiently clear in the production.

"They did not understand that Chris was trampling

blankets in the tub. They thought she was cooling her feet! And they could not understand why her mother should want to commit suicide, when she had her family and so much around her that seemed worth living for.

"I don't think the 'trauchle' of the farmer's wife was brought out, though they did imply that she was pregnant again. Otherwise I enjoyed it thoroughly."

Her daughter Rhea (41), whose husband is an invalid, is a law lecturer at Hatfield Polytechnic and son Daryll is a sales director in Worcester.

In their English homes they viewed with great pride and satisfaction, heart-strings tugged towards the land of the Mearns where it all happened.

Despite the criticisms, I am hopeful of the television series. To those who watch it, I would say—follow up the experience by reading it. And then give me hell if it does not deeply and permanently enrich your life!

MY FATHER

The fact that I made my first appearance in the world that morning did nothing to disturb the peace or warmth of a July day in 1931, as cattle wended their way to the weekly market at Maud, in Aberdeenshire.

Even my father managed to absorb the information when it was brought to him in his auctioneer's rostrum and to continue selling bullocks, with no more sense of occasion than if a hen had just laid an egg.

Not that he didn't care. For my father has been caring all his life—caring about the land and the people who wrest a living from it, about the quality of their existence and the heritage which they try to preserve.

For more than 40 years, in fact, the North-East corner of Scotland—the heartland of Aberdeenshire beef—has been his parish, as livestock auctioneer and valuator, friend and adviser to the struggling crofter no less than to the man of acres.

John Webster has been a name in the farming community, a rumbustious and rugged individualist whose honesty and forthrightness compel him to call a spade a spade on polite occasions—and "a bloody shovel" whenever possible.

115

Many a young auctioneer who quivered at his boom has lived to thank him for guidance and discipline. His humour is widely known, not least by the dear lady who wrote to sympathise with him for having "a measle".

"A measle?" he bellowed his full-moon face glowing with red spots. "Ah've thoosans o' the b.....!"

He belongs to a breed that believes the world begins to disintegrate somewhere south of Stonehaven—and that by the time you reach London you might as well have gone to hell.

Yet none of it conflicts with the fact that he is a solid elder of the Aul' Kirk, for, in all truth, there are few finer human beings.

Left as head of the family at eight, when his father contracted anthrax from an animal and died, he soon left school and graduated from herd laddie to market clerk and then to young auctioneer, scouring the countryside on his motor-bike, persuading farmers to send their cattle to his mart.

Such was his vitality and knowledge—and memory—that he was once reputed to know every farm and croft in the 1,000 square miles of Buchan, its occupant, acreage and stock potential.

People in authority say this knowledge of beef farming, acquired without book or tutor, is unsurpassed. Within the framework of his humour he has a special corner of tolerance for the "educated ostrich" whose worth he more often compares unfavourably with that of the humble crofter.

I have not written about my father before and the only reason I do so now is that in this, the week of his 65th birthday, he retires from the auction ring, pretty well undefeated.

It has been an eventful career, from the days of the shelt and gig, the paraffin lamp and fine, warm friendliness, through to an age when the machine has come to till the land and help transplant rural folk in the alien environs of the city.

What they call progress continues, with the Government prodding the small farmer to get out and hand over to the bigger combines. I asked my father for his observations.

"The tycoons and the big groups have come to run the land and it is not a particularly good development," he says. "The small farmer and his wife have been the backbone of British agriculture. They were not there for big profits but to earn a living and to shape a way of life for their children and themselves.

"A lot depended on the wife and what she could earn from eggs. But it has become so uneconomical to produce eggs—and there are so many other handicaps—that the same couple find they can be better off on an employee's wage.

"For the work they do, that should never happen. They are good useful citizens, rearing healthy children, who in turn carry on the tradition.

"They are being driven to the already-congested areas and the social life of the countryside is going with them.

"Farming is still a way of life I would recommend. But you need capital, which is hard to get. You need a lot of hard work. And the job is being tied-up in too much damned red tape."

With these few words, my father will withdraw to his farm on the braes of Honeyneuk, overlooking the village, from which his gusty personality will still radiate over Buchan.

From putting through 40,000 cattle a year at the local marts—he called for his last bid yesterday—he will content himself with supervising his own acres, having first risked a "sair cowpin" on the Atlantic to see how they are managing to run Canada.

I write, of course, as the errant only son, who didn't stay

to farm but went off in the late forties to a 'tuppence-ha'penny job' on a newspaper.

The sin was almost unforgivable. Except that my mother notices him reading my articles more than once and hears him telling people that "the loon is daein' nae sae bad".

That's my father!

LAUGHTER IN COURT . . .
FROM THE BLUE JOKE-BOOK

——————————— *22nd April 1970* ———————————

Two youths who appeared in Glasgow Sheriff Court yesterday for breaking into Ibrox Park found that the place is not without its sense of humour.

In answer to a lawyer who hoped that the accused were not in pursuit of trophies, Sheriff Francis Middleton looked over his gold-rimmed specs and said: "I agree. That is not the place to break into for that!"

The shaft of wit is not in isolation.

Indeed it is symptomatic of the football public's current attitude to the mighty institution of Rangers Football Club as it strives to restore the balance which has been lost to the traditional rivals of Celtic Park.

Jokes abound—and the Rangers' supporters themselves are leading the fashion, as if to show that they can at least retain a sense of humour through their club's unsettled period of renovation and spring-clean.

They button you in the street, in the pub or at the workbench to brighten their end-of-season doldrums with a smile at the Rangers' expense. Some are fresh and some are adaptations of earlier football jokes.

"Heard about Rangers last week?" they'll ask with a

119

twinkle. Of course you haven't. "They won the toss—and celebrated with a lap of honour!"

Another blue-nose chips in with the one about the dustbins. "Rangers heard that Jock Stein used dustbins so that his players can practise mazy runs. They decided to copy the method. The manager sent for a progress report and got it—the dustbins are winning 2-1!"

"Heard about the Rangers goalkeeper who had just been told he was no longer wanted at Ibrox. He rushed out of the stadium in a distraught state, dived to catch a bus—but it passed under him."

Up pipes another wag with an adjusted version of the kind of story they used to tell about Partick Thistle.

A man phoned Ibrox to ask what time the game started. A polite gentleman at the other end gave him his answer: "What time suits you, sir?"

Managers' names have never been able to escape the pun. Rangers were for long said to be the cleanest team in Scotland, if only by virtue of the fact that they were White-washed and Symon-ised.

Now they are asking why they signed Donald Duck. And the answer is: "To help Willie Waddell."

And last week one of the Apollo 13 astronauts is said to have shrugged off difficulties and dangers by remarking: "Thank goodness I'm not in Willie Waddell's shoes."

We have all heard that silverware experts invariably put more value on the Rangers' trophy collection than on the Celtic one—because they are all antiques!

But the latest story brings us back to dwindling crowds. It is one which manager Waddell will no doubt accept as his challenge for the season ahead.

At an end-of-the-season game, says the story, the loud-speaker burst into action with this pre-match announcement: "Here, for the benefit of the team, is a list of the spectators!"

ENJOY YOURSELVES! SAID THE QUEEN
—AND WE DID

—————————— *7th July 1970* ——————————

With the ancient boom of gunfire, the modern scream of jet airplanes and quite the most magnificent display of colour, precision and military music that Scotland has ever seen, the Ninth British Commonwealth Games were opened at Meadowbank Sports Centre last night by Prince Philip, who flew in from Canada for the occasion.

And what a spectacle of panchromatic splendour it was! The pomp, the majesty, the humanity—all were there.

And a reminder came in Her Majesty the Queen's message that this was an occasion to enjoy and to use for the cementing of better understanding.

What a day this was for Auld Scotia, having given so ungrudgingly of her sons and her skills to every corner of the earth and now pulling back the threads of Commonwealth into a magnificent tapestry of colour and warmth and friendship.

The greatest family in the world had come this day to the mother table.

And as the feast began amid scenes of joy, I wondered what kind of creature could stay unmoved by an occasion like this. Few did.

Long before the start, the 25,000 crowd had begun its build-up of anticipation.

Then, at precisely 4pm, into the emptiness of the arena came the Guard of Honour.

They were the men of the Queen's Own Highlanders, the public duties battalion in Edinburgh, headed by their pipes and drums and wheeling in splendid order, white spats gleaming and bayonets sparkling.

They raised the flags—the Union Jack, the flag of Jamaica and the Scottish Saltire.

The crowd, dressed in a gaily coloured mixture of summer shades, cheered in infectious waves of enthusiasm.

They renewed it as the royal limousine drove on to the track and Prince Philip waved his way round on one lap before stepping out to be greeted by Lord Provost McKay of Edinburgh and Mr Alexander Ross, chairman of the British Commonwealth Games Federation.

Prince Philip shook hands with his left, his right hand still strapped up from his polo fall.

The guns boomed out from the distance of Holyrood Park and the military band struck up God Save the Queen.

On the very last bar—just as the programme had forecast—the scream of 12 jet planes, Lightnings and Phantoms from Leuchars, materialised from nowhere.

The crowd cheered the incredible precision—surely as fine a demonstration as there has ever been of the British aptitude for organising the grand occasion.

Prince Philip inspected his guard before they marched out to the rousing strains of "Scotland the Brave".

No sooner had they gone than the massed bands came swinging into the arena, the six drum majors, resplendent in feather bonnets and leading their men with maces flying.

The whole show of 200 men weaved intricate patterns of formation until they fanned out in a welcome for the 128

Highland dancers who stepped smartly out in their varied kilts and tunics.

The bands were those of the Royal Scots Greys, the Black Watch, the Queen's Own Highlanders, the 52nd Lowland Volunteers and the Police Bands of Glasgow, Edinburgh, Aberdeen and Dundee.

The massed military bands were next to add to the spectacle, the red tunics of the Scots Guards separating the white helmets of the Royal Marines from the blue caps of the Royal Air Force, and all flanked by the Greys, the Black Watch and the Queen's Own Highlanders.

The Royal Scottish Dance Society brought the sun with their arrival, as well as a show of grace and beauty which thrilled the crowd, their menfolk in kilts and their ladies in long white dresses and tartan sashes.

Back came the pipes and drums to interweave and inter-play with trombones and euphoniums, the amalgam to play their way out once more with "Scotland the Brave" and rhythmic clapping of an enraptured audience echoing across the stadium.

Then came the opening proper and the parade of athletes, all 2,000 of them from 42 different countries.

They were led by Jamaica, the island in the sun, hosts of 1966. Thereafter they came in alphabetical order from Antigua and Australia right through to Wales and Zambia, each group of competitors in its own distinctive and pictur-esque uniform.

The greens and yellows of the Australians contrasted with the brilliant red of the Canadians and blue of the Scots.

There was a special cheer for little Miss Badra, carrying the banner as Ceylon's only competitor.

Prince Philip stood on the brilliant blue dais as each country passed, lowering its flag in royal salute as it came.

What a day for Private George Geddes from Rosemarkie,

123

a young Queen's Own Highlander who had the honour of leading the Jamaican team and therefore the entire parade.

With Prince Philip on the dais was a man whose heart must surely have swelled with justifiable pride—Sir Herbert Brechin, former Lord Provost of Edinburgh, the man who refused to give up in his 15-year fight to bring the Games to Edinburgh. There before his very eyes was the dream in reality.

On they came in waves to the mounting cheers and roars of an ecstatic crowd.

One of Kenya's competitors, determined to make the most of his big day, strutted out with an exaggerated step and a massive grin on his face, raising peals of laughter.

Hogan Kid Bassey, the former boxing champion, now training the Nigerians, was also cheered as was the Welsh standard bearer, the mountainous Terry Perdue, who appropriate for a weight lifter, carried the heavy banner with one hand.

Special applause was reserved for the Scottish team bringing up the rear as hosts and led by Alexander Leckie, the fencer.

The teams formed up in the centre of the stadium for the arrival of the Queen's message, which had started its journey appropriately in Canada, where her Majesty has been touring and where the first Commonwealth Games were held in 1930.

In it she stressed the founding spirit which was that "they shall be merrier and less stern and will substitute the stimulus of a novel adventure for the pressure of international rivalry."

She added: "These words should be remembered. I hope that all who have come together at Edinburgh from all parts of the world will first and foremost enjoy themselves.

"I hope, too, that both the competitions and the social

events will encourage new friendships and a better understanding of the Commonwealth as a free association of people of good will."

The message had come in a silver baton by air and relay runners.

The last lap was left to 1966 marathon champion Jim Alder of Scotland.

He circled the track before handing the baton to Prince Philip, who read the message and declared the Games open.

The flag was raised and 5,000 pigeons released as Crawford Fairbrother, the Scottish high jumper, stepped forward to take the oath on behalf of the athletes. He said:

"We declare that we will take part in the British Commonwealth Games of 1970 in the spirit of true sportsmanship, recognising the rules which govern them and desirous of participating in them for the honour of our Commonwealth and for the glory of sport."

With that, Prince Philip boarded his car and drove out of the stadium, followed by the 2,000 competitors and the massed bands.

If this memorable opening is a foretaste of things to come, what an event we have in our midst!

Much greater, I suspect, than even the most optimistic and imaginative of us have bargained for.

BUD NEILL DIES AT 59

————————— *29th August 1970* —————————

Bud Neill, that wonderfully off-beat and warmly human genius of the topical cartoon, died yesterday at his home in Glenrothes, Fife, aged 59.

Over many years, his daily drawings delighted readers of the *Scottish Daily Express*. For the big, awkward frame of Bud Neill was really an observation post for the Scottish scene.

His eyes and ears were aerials for our special characteristics. And his hands were the instruments of translating the conclusions of a keenly understanding mind.

Through the apparent zaniness of his drawings and captions there filtered the unmistakeable truths about our strengths and stupidities, our wiles and weaknesses.

The unconventional nature of Bud Neill's art was also an expression of his wildly individualistic self.

For Bud, who was born William Neill, in the Patrick district of Glasgow, had been an Alexanders' bus driver in the West of Scotland, a soldier, a funeral undertaker and a professional harmonica player in Canada.

His conventional home was in Glenrothes but he spent a large part of his week in a converted post office at Halbeath, in another part of Fife, where he pursued his art in mildly hermit surroundings.

With a subtlety of expression, a hotch-potch of emotions and the melancholic look of a clown, he acquired an aura of mystery, heightened by blue-tinted spectacles which he used as a corrective of the blues and greens in his mild form of colour-blindness.

Behind those blue shutters he absorbed the human scene and like to poke fun at it, even through his own fashions. He liked to comb his hair forward and latterly was playing with a Skinhead style.

It was all quiet fun with Bud. Even when I was talking to him a few months ago he had me in stitches over his loss of memory. But it was no joke. And maybe Bud knew it.

That brain which bubbled with good humour was also developing a tumour. They operated but the days of Bud Neill were numbered. In recent weeks he had been in a semi-comatose state.

He leaves his wife, three sons and a daughter. And he leaves a wealth of memories.

Perhaps his most-quoted caption-verse (it was not his own favourite) was printed under the bedraggled Glasgow character standing at a bus stop on a cold, cold night:

> Winter's came
> The snow has fell
> Wee Josi's nosis frozis well;
> Wee Josi's frozis nosis skintit,
> Winter's diabolic—intit?

Bud Neill added to human happiness. And what better epitaph could any man wish for?

127

WHY LEX WILL BE TAKING
THE LAST LAUGH

—————————— *12th October 1970* ——————————

You can take way the tram-cars and obliterate the Gorbals; you can seal off Sauchiehall Street and put puffers up in smoke. But there's a limit to the amount of destruction you can inflict on the sacred institutions.

And, if they can seek an Act of Parliament in Brazil to stop the transfer of that great footballer, Pele, to another country, then I am certain the people of Glasgow will consider some such drastic step over the case of Alexander McLean Cameron, who abbreviates himself to Lex McLean.

The news to bring quivering torsos to a standstill is that the incomparable Lex McLean show, covering a five-month summer season at the Pavilion Theatre, Glasgow, since the mid-fifties, is coming off at the end of this week.

It has nothing to do with the decline of the theatre, for the legendary Lex plays to 18,000 people every week, packing them in with a brand of humour which has earned him all the superlatives of success and proves that there is still an audience for the music hall if the performer is good enough.

He will star in a *Five Past Eight* show in Edinburgh next summer and follow it with a short season in Glasgow. But

128

the old pattern, which has just seen him in a 22-week run at the Pavilion, with two shows a night, is over.

His contract ran out last year, he continued without one and now despite an offer of higher percentages, he has said: "No thanks. I have had enough of the stress and the worry. I've decided that it is no use working and paying tax until ye drap deid."

At his luxurious villa in Helensburgh yesterday, Lex explained some of the difficulties:

"New material is the main part of it. You must keep up your standards. The audience demands it. You must also keep up with the times and stay topical— and it all gets difficult when you have been running in Glasgow for as long as I have.

"I have to do most of the material myself because there are no writers around. I get humorous scripts sent to me but people won't necessarily laugh at humour, even if it looks good on paper.

"You've got to add spice and punch to it. Comedy goes in cycles. We had the humour of George West and Dave Willis, for example, but people wouldn't laugh at that now."

Lex McLean, who earns handsomely, runs a Mercedes and refreshes himself in Spain, has gained the popular description of "Sexy Lexy" and not for nothing.

Yet he gets touchy if you brand his humour as "blue".

"I'm not a blue comedian nor an obscene one, just broad. I mean to say, when you compare my material with some of the muck you hear today . . .

"One critic who once said I would need an X certificate later said that *Hair* was worth seeing. Well, to me, *Hair* is just pure, unadulterated fifth. The show which I put on is, I reckon, the best 9s. 6d. worth in Britain today."

There are plenty ready to endorse the view, for McLean is the complete professional trouper.

He emerged after the war playing piano, saxophone and bagpipes, "feeding" other comedians but very quickly drawing more laughs for himself.

He knew his people and their humour. It had to do with honeymoon couples and drunks and fanatical football supporters.

He was, and has remained, in touch with those around him, catering for the ever present need of ordinary folk everywhere—to enjoy themselves with a good, hearty belly-laugh, preferably in the warmth and intimacy of a live theatre.

In all the lofty talk about culture, it is easy to forget that it is really a multi-coloured creature. Lex McLean has looked after a side of it which is too often ignored.

LET ME TELL YOU ABOUT A MOTHER

———————— *25th December 1970* ————————

In this Christmas week of toys and tinsel, when we shall meet in our family gatherings and perhaps refresh ourselves on the greatest story of them all, is there a better time in the year to pause awhile and take stock?

There are moments in the modern rush when progress would seem to go backwards, when the machine means more and people mean less, when the simple courtesies evaporate and create a longing for the days when the warmth of neighbourliness made up for the material wants of a less-affluent time.

Perhaps the recent bread strike and power cuts have taught us something. They rekindled a spirit of the war years when the barriers of smugness or mere reticence were swept aside by people talking to each other.

I believe we should look around, not just this week but every week—not just during a bread strike or a power cut— and consider those who might appreciate our help, or even our kindly word or pleasant smile. They can be counted in millions.

Today I am thinking about a Scotswoman who nearly died when her only child was born. For weeks she lay in hospital, set aside as being beyond help, but willing herself to live for the sake of the child.

She won. And she cared for her son and reared him and sent him out into the world and took a pride in him.

And I doubt if that son ever as much as expressed his appreciation or his love, for the tender word comes alien to the lips of so many Scots.

Today that same woman lies once more in Aberdeen Royal Infirmary, barely knowing where she is but fighting every inch to stay back from death's door.

And that negligent son would give so much to have a second chance—to be able to put right that debt of gratitude which so many of us fail to pay.

The moral of that story this Christmas week is simply that we should not require the second chance. For the sake of others, as well as for our own peace of mind, we should grasp that abundance of opportunity to get it right the first time.

If you were tempted to think that the story of the negligent son is a hypothetical one, you would be wrong. I can vouch for every strand of his thoughts and feelings.

For I am talking about myself.

PS: Sadly, my mother died three weeks later, aged 64.

A BAD OMEN,
SAID THE WORRIED KING

26th December 1970

The sudden appearance of a lump of stone outside Parliament House in Edinburgh, with the claim that it is the real Stone of Destiny, stirs up afresh one of the great romantic dramas of modern Scottish history.

For the simple act of yesterday morning took place exactly 20 years to the Christmas Day when the headlines of the world proclaimed that this famous symbol of Scottish independence had been stolen from under the Coronation Chair in Westminster Abbey.

Four young Scots had succeeded in removing this massive chunk of masonry, eventually to return it to what they considered its rightful resting-place of Scotland.

The Stone was reproduced 108 days later at the ancient Arbroath Abbey. But all hopes that it would be allowed to stay in Scotland were dashed by the police. They could not get it back to Westminster Abbey quick enough.

But there are at least two replicas (one in a Glasgow sculptor's yard) and the question arises as to whether the real Stone was returned.

Was it retained in case the Government decided against leaving it in Scotland?

133

Is this now a second replica, produced to test official reaction 20 years later, with the real Stone still hidden?

Is it an attempt to stimulate interest in nationalism?

Or is it just a ploy?

Whatever the truth of it, the happening in Edinburgh yesterday rather vividly brings back, like a fiery dream, the excitement of that day in 1950 when the imagination of people everywhere was stirred by the dramatic events which upset the gaitered glory of Westminster.

And what was it all about anyway?

To start with, the Stone of Scone, as it is known in Scotland, had long been a matter of contention between the Scots and the English. More than 650 years had passed since Edward I of England, who had reached as far as Elgin, returned south, victorious with the stone on which the kings of the Scots had long been crowned.

According to legend, it is the Stone on which Jacob rested his head when he saw the vision of the angels ascending and descending the ladder. It is believed that it was brought to Scotland by Scota, daughter of a Pharaoh.

Edward's motive was to deprive the Scots of this symbol of their independence and to show where authority over Scotland lay.

So to 1950, five years after war's end and a dreary spell of post-war austerity in which nationalism had begun to reassert itself in Scotland yet again in a way that was to develop along such guerrilla lines as the blowing up of post-boxes.

Then, out of the blue, came "The Stone". A Glasgow student called Ian Hamilton masterminded the event which, far from being a student prank, was the outcome of deeply-held convictions about the rights of the Scottish people.

Hamilton "cased the joint" then teamed up with two other Glasgow students, Gavin Vernon and Alan Stuart, and a

Wester Ross schoolteacher, Kay Matheson, to carry out the plan.

Off to London they went by car. The first intention was for Hamilton to conceal himself inside the Abbey at closing time, but he was discovered and beat a hasty retreat.

It could only be done by forcing an entry. With Kay Matheson lying handy with the Ford Anglia, the three men used a jemmy to enter Westminster Abbey.

The Stone was almost out of the Abbey when a policeman spotted the car, came up to enquire—and Ian Hamilton and Kay Matheson promptly enacted a love scene to divert him!

Like a John Buchan drama, the Stone was carried clear of London, buried at Rochester in Kent, and eventually brought to Scotland on the Hogmanay Night.

In the following April it turned up at Arbroath Abbey.

Despite the calls to have it kept in Scotland, the Stone— if it be the real Stone—went back to Westminster Abbey.

Before the Stone finally turned up at Arbroath, it was known that the authorities were desperately anxious about its whereabouts.

The matter was discussed at the highest level. The then Secretary of State for Scotland, the late Hector McNeil, made no secret of the anxiety of the late King George VI.

Says Mr Sandy Trotter, at that time editor of the *Scottish Daily Express*: "Mr McNeil told me that the King regarded the Stone's disappearance as a bad omen and was worried about it."

Many eminent men eagerly donned cloaks-and-daggers in secret negotiations with those whom they believed could secure the return of the Stone.

By that time the four students were widely known—and were being closely watched by the police. They had no idea where the Stone was.

In the thick of the plot were the Nationalist leader, Dr

John MacCormick, then Rector of Glasgow University, and his close friend, Councillor Robert Gray, a monumental sculptor.

It is believed that they finally decided that Arbroath Abbey would be an appropriate resting place—with its links with the historic and splendid Declaration of Independence of 1320.

Nationalist feeling issued a dramatic reminder of its existence. The years that followed were to bring it a respectability and acceptance which manifested itself in the 1967 election of Mrs Winnie Ewing to Parliament as M.P. for Hamilton.

Scotland enthused in rebellion against the slights of centuries. The graph of interest went up and the graph, I suspect, came down again rather sharply. This latest episode at least keeps the subject in the picture.

And the Stone of Destiny lies somewhere.

The question that authority must ponder today is: But where?

WHEN YOU LIVE WITH THE HORROR OF KILLING A MAN

——————— *31st December 1970* ———————

Calum Finlayson eased his large, athletic frame into a chair, pondered the events of a hot, summer's day in 1969 and gave me a graphic description of how he raised a revolver and fired the shot which killed a man.

That bullet wrote his name into the history books as the first policeman in Scotland to fire a fatal shot.

As a chief superintendent in Glasgow City Police, it fell to Calum Finlayson to decide, on a tenement landing in Kay Street, Springburn, what to do about heavily-armed James Griffiths, dangerous and wanted criminal from England, who had already sprayed gunshot into 13 innocent people within an hour and was still firing away crazily.

Today the gallant policeman, with a Skye parentage and an almost gentle manner, can open his heart and tell me:

"I thought a lot about the fact that I had killed a man. But any qualms I had with my conscience were cleared by the support I got from my colleagues."

And he can say it now—in contrast to the silence of the time—because he leaves the police force this weekend, aged 59, to take up a top security job with Ronald Lyon Estates Ltd.

137

"I knew that inside that tenement flat there was a man armed to the teeth and intending to kill. It was the point of no return and I had to do something. In my position I made my decision for the protection of the public and my colleague, Detective Sergeant Ian Smith, and myself.

"It was a warm day and I was perspiring and excited but I was not afraid. I knew that Griffiths had a rifle and a sawn-off shotgun and I knew the devastating effect of the latter.

"I said: 'If he gets us on the stairhead, he will blow our heads off.' Using the door as a shield, I opened the letter-box and looked through. I could hear him shooting out but couldn't see him. The lobby was strewn with broken glass.

"Then I noticed his shadow coming—and there was Griffiths, turning in towards the kitchen with the rifle at the raised position, the shotgun under his arm and two bandoliers of ammunition round his waist and shoulders. I think he had seen me at the letter-box because he stopped and looked at the door. It was then that I had to make my decision. It was either Griffiths or Ian Smith and myself.

"I decided to fire and try to maim and disarm him. So I raised the revolver to the letter-box and took aim at his shoulder. We were about to spring and grapple with him when he suddenly fired at the door.

"I called to Ian 'My God, I've missed him!' Then we heard the clatter on the floor and we sprang. He had dropped to his knees. I had not aimed to kill but the bullet had ricocheted down from his shoulder towards his heart, mortally wounding him. Ian Smith took him down the stair but I think he was dead before we got to the bottom."

As the sound of gunfire died away a terrorised city came out of its hiding and the whole nightmarish story began to piece itself together.

James Griffiths, a well-known criminal from Rochdale who was staying in digs in Glasgow, was wanted as a suspect in the murder of Mrs Rachel Ross in Ayr the previous week.

On that warm afternoon of July 15, Regional Crime Squad men had gone to interview him at his digs in Holyrood Crescent, just off Glasgow's Great Western Road.

He received them with gunfire, wounding a policeman in the back, then blasting down into the street. Calum Finlayson takes up the story:

"It happened in my division and I was at the office when I heard of calls for assistance. I arrived at the scene unarmed but, in collaboration with Detective Chief Superintendent Tom Goodall, decided that whoever approached the man should be armed.

"We laid siege on the house and he kept on firing from the window. All traffic was stopped and the public cleared from the area. Then he escaped from the house through the rear, commandeered a car at gunpoint and drove off across town.

"I was with Superintendent James Binnie but we lost contact with him. Then we learned that he had crashed the car, demanded a bottle of brandy, again at gunpoint, in the Round Toll Bar, and shot a newsvendor, who later died.

"He commandeered a lorry and eventually turned up in Kay Street, where he was firing from a tenement window, wounding a child who was playing outside.

"There was nothing but the sound of screaming cars as the police closed in. Again I came on the scene and, arming myself, made my way cautiously up Kay Street, keeping under cover till I came to the last close, where my colleague Detective Sergeant Smith, who was also armed was waiting."

When the dust had settled and they had buried Griffiths in a grave at the Linn Cemetery, the identity of the policeman who performed the duty of ending the life of a killer-at-large was not revealed. Calum Finlayson had enough to cope with at that moment.

139

It was not until last month that he went to Buckingham Palace with his wife Catriona to collect his M.B.E. from the Queen. With him, appropriately, was Ian Smith, who received the B.E.M.

As spectators began to leave the Rangers-Celtic match on 2nd January 1971, a last-minute equalising goal brought ecstasy at the Rangers end. But it also brought a swirl of movement and, in the crush and confusion, the crowd collapsed down an exit stairway. It was stairway No.13—and 66 people lay dead.

THE IBROX DISASTER

—————————— *4th January 1971* ——————————

The build-up to the Ibrox Disaster came on a fine afternoon of winter-red sun, always threatened by the haze which would eventually close in around four o'clock.

It was a day for getting to the stadium early if, like me, you had no ticket for an all-ticket game. I parked the car half-a-mile from Ibrox Stadium and walked briskly towards the mighty, red-bricked edifice which proclaims that this is the home of Rangers Football Club.

I went in anticipation of finding someone with a ticket to spare, but as I approached the ground shortly after 2pm, the overriding impression was one of incredible hush.

For an occasion which is generally hailed as "the greatest club game in the world" (a description restated in the official programme on Saturday) this Rangers-Celtic encounter was enjoying the most peaceful preamble I can remember for a big game.

Gradually, however, the atmosphere built up. Around the main entrance the pre-match electricity began to generate that feeling of excitement as players and other personalities appeared and disappeared, as New Year greetings were exchanged and necks were craned in search of friends who would come to collect their tickets.

Almost inevitably there would be the spare ticket, and at 2.45 I landed lucky. A friend had not turned up and this chap could sell me one—for what turned out to be the disaster end of the ground.

I paid him his six shillings and headed in the direction of the fatal passageway. But perhaps there is a design in things.

For, at the last minute, I bumped into a friend who must have been about the only man at Ibrox with a grandstand ticket to spare. I accepted, turned to the first ticketless fan in view and resold my terracing voucher.

He was delighted. I can only hope that I did not sell him a ticket to tragedy.

Inside the ground 80,000 people had settled comfortably for a game with clearcut issues. Reigning League champions Celtic needed both points to keep on the heels of Aberdeen, who are striding ahead of them.

For Rangers' fans, the championship might be a forlorn hope but, if only they could beat old rivals Celtic, the world would be a more tolerable place to live in.

As you sit in the grandstand, looking northwards on to the pitch, the traditionally Celtic end is to the left and the Rangers' end to the right. It was at that far-right corner that death was soon to run riot.

But now was not the time for tragedy. Now was for excitement, for a game of desperate endeavour to inflict defeat within the greatest rivalry football has ever known.

For certain, it was one of the best-behaved crowds we have ever seen at an Old Firm game.

In the fading light of half-time, the blue floodlights came filtering through in a ghostly shimmer and it was then that I experienced one of those feelings that you can put down to premonition, ultra-sensitivity or perhaps just a journalist's hunch.

I was there on a day-off, as a spectator, but I consciously asked myself if, in the event of something happening here today, I had absorbed enough of the atmosphere to write about it. So I looked around for the sights and sounds.

I also decided to leave a few minutes before the end. The confusing roar of that last dramatic minute came loud and clear as I walked back to the car.

The sheer joy of the Rangers fans over the equalising goal had torn into the magnifying mists of an evening which was quickly losing its crescent moon and glorious horizon.

Four-forty p.m. still looked as good a time as any for life and laughter. It takes only seconds for the hush and the horror and the utter silence of death to descend.

I DON'T CARE WHO WINS,
AS LONG AS IT'S THE DONS

—————————— *17th April 1971* ——————————

The massive trek is on this morning. From all corners of
Scotland they are homing in on the Northern Lights of Old
Aberdeen for the match which will virtually decide whether
Aberdeen or Celtic are the football champions of Scotland
for season 1970-71.

About 20,000 green-and-white Glaswegians will invade
the Silver City to mingle with a further 25,000 Aberdonians
coming from a' the airts in anticipation of a memorable
spectacular.

And that is only about half the number who want tickets.

A dozen enthusiasts from the Aberdeenshire market town
of Turriff were setting out at 2am, after a dance, to cover
the 36 miles to Aberdeen as a sponsored walk.

It is typical of the fever which is gripping this North-East
corner.

For fanatical idiocy, I may well qualify for the special
award. As an exiled Aberdonian, I came back home a full
week in advance. After all, you can get caught in traffic jams!

I have always been a sucker for the pre-match
atmosphere, as well as an Aberdeen supporter of incurable
and uncamouflaged bias.

Since 1942 you are liable to have found me hanging around Pittodrie Park waiting for a glimpse of every hero from Jock Pattillo, George Hamilton and Ernie Waldron through to the current race of stars.

There are Press cuttings to show me as a schoolboy heading the queue for autographs when Aberdeen beat Rangers in the League Cup final of 1946.

Around that time I had a special admiration for a certain Martin Buchan, the Dons player who was to become the father of two more Dons, Martin and George Buchan, of the present-day team.

Nowadays I am joined in my fanaticism by three young Websters who, by some miraculous means, have also become Aberdeen supporters, though living in Glasgow.

No coercion, no bullying. Just a simple explanation that, if I feed them and clothe them, there is a little matter of loyalty to be considered. All very reasonable.

We have been in Aberdeenshire all week, absorbing the atmosphere that spreads from Union Street outwards to a North-East countryside where soccer has overtaken seed time as a topic of conversation.

And we are equipped with those precious tickets which are as scarce as Aberdonians on the proverbial flag day. (On the latter score, I need hardly reiterate the denial of Aberdonian meanness. How can we help it if we are born with short arms and low pockets?)

What matters is that our hearts are in the right place. Nor should our voices be lacking as the all-red men of Pittodrie run out this afternoon to meet the might of Glasgow Celtic who have won the League Championship for the past five years.

The Dons, who beat Celtic for the Scottish Cup last year, have not won the league since 1955.

That is one good reason why I'll be out there this

afternoon, waving my rattle to deafen the opposition.

PS: Celtic won the Championship—and went on to make it nine in a row!

A WOMAN'S WRATH

—————————— *25th June 1971* ——— —————

If you are looking for the most ferocious political animal in Scotland today you need go no further than Janey Buchan, Glasgow bailie, wife of Norman (a Scottish Under-Secretary in the Wilson Government) and herself a woman with an eye on Westminster.

For Janey is an old-time Socialist hell-raiser, a sock-it-to-'em girl who admits to revelling in the class struggle.

At the weekend she raised shivers by refusing to wear her robes of office at Archbishop Scanlan's jubilee.

She opened her smoke-free lungs yesterday in a major battle at Glasgow City Chambers, to have smoking banned in theatres, public halls, buses and so on.

In between times I managed to pin her down to a session of self-examination, a venom-venting ramble in which we explored what it is that puts the tick into Janey Buchan's time-bombs.

She is 44: daughter of a tram-car driver; was brought up in Partick; still stays there—and who would dare shift her?

Political opponents give her a wide berth. Labour colleagues find her an uncomfortable bed-fellow. Most men take one look at her public image and consider that the missus isn't so bad after all.

But Janey, once described as "the Boadicea of the Glasgow Left," battles on, grinding the spikes of her chariot into those she feels deserves them.

She has a broad mind and beautiful complexion, but there are certain four-letter words she finds offensive. Like "Tory". You say it, and then act as if you had burped.

For if Janey refrains from comparing Tories to rats in a sewer it is purely out of respect for the rats.

"I hate them!" she spits, curling her legs on a sofa. "If I were a religious person, which I'm not, I would find original sin spelled out in the Tory party. And working-class Tories! They just about send me up the wall."

"You're an aggressive woman," I ventured, with a stab at the obvious.

"Yes, I'm aggressive, but I hope for the right reasons. Mind you, it surprises me that I have this reputation for being a toad-faced old bitch. Because that is not so.

"I'll tell you a story though. The woman who comes to help me has a little boy who was describing me to his sister. He had noticed my habit of going about the house in bare feet and he said: 'Ye'll know her because she's a big wumman wi' grey hair and she walks aboot like Tarzan!' You can never get any illusions about yourself in Glasgow."

If Janey needs a saving grace—and many believe she does—then it is her well-developed sense of humour.

"But I'll tell you the kind of thing that makes me aggressive. Last week I went to see Lady Tweedsmuir (Minister of State at the Scottish Office) about the U.C.S. crisis.

"Now there she was, a gracious Tory lady, but she didn't seem to know . . . and quite honestly, it wouldn't have taken much for me to be quite violent towards her.

"I can feel very aggressive towards jumped-up Johnnies."

"Have you ever struck anyone?" I asked at a safe distance.

above: Field-Marshal
Montgomery looks on
as General Kinzel signs
the German surrender,
May 4th 1945

left:
Richard Rodgers

opposite above: Robert Boothby, Fay Compton and Compton MacKenzie

opposite below: Bud Neill

above: Jim Baxter

right: Lex MacLean

left: Maxwell Garvie,
murder victim

below: Mrs Garvie
and her accomplice,
Brian Tevendale

above: Millicent Martin, star of *That Was The Week That Was*

above: Robert Graves, celebrated author of *Goodbye To All That*

above: John Banks,
Glasgow bookmaker

right: Jock Stein

above: Mick Jagger, Sixties icon

"Only my son. But there are things which make me feel violent. You see, Scotland is a terribly philistine country, with all this 'Wha's like us?' stuff. I mean, people are so pleased with rubbish.

"Take poetry. Right? The number of people in Scotland who have thought that they could write poetry, and were so pleased with it, is quite amazing. Somebody should have punched them between the eyes.

"Now take the collection of poems written at the time of Edward VII's death. I'll read some of it to you . . . now isn't that no' terrible? I can get quite violent about that kind of stuff. In fact, I'm thinking of putting on 'An Evening of Scottish Rubbish'.

"My relationship with this country is a love-hate one. I love the Glesca cheekiness, the humour. One of the greatest artists Scotland ever had was Bud Neill.

"The people of Glasgow can never resist getting the boot in, can they?"

"Does all this hate not tend to corrode your character?" I asked.

"On the contrary, it makes it," she replies.

"Why do you bother to take a determined stand on such harmless trappings as a bailie's robes?" I asked. "Don't you overdo it?"

"There is nothing virtuous in being against robes but I think they are faintly ludicrous and I'll never wear them. You see, I'm a strong traditionalist for worthwhile tradition. I believe symbols are important but we get all steamed up about the wrong symbols, such as tartan, which is, by and large, spurious.

"Anyway, there's a time for losing your dignity and saying 'To hell with it!'

"I hope I am not aggressive in private life. I know some people see me and say 'poor Norman'—but he's an untidy person and, I think, lucky to be married to me.

"He never gives me a birthday present because he knows it would be a waste of time. I wouldn't want it."

Norman and Janey met when he handed her a Young Communist League leaflet at a street corner. They married in the year of peace, 1945, and now have a married son themselves.

When they celebrated their silver wedding last year, they asked their friends to give money for a family of children they help to support in South Africa. They raised £380.

Janey remembers her parents doing the same thing for Spanish refugees during the Civil War of 1937.

She may overreact to life, but the heat of her anger overflows to a warmth of personality which she somehow manages to hide in her public life. I suspect it embarrasses her.

Pert, provocative, pugnacious she certainly is. But add to that incorruptibly honest.

Honest to the point of telling me that Norman went out for the last May Day parade, laid down his new £38 coat somewhere and came home without it.

"A £38 coat?" I queried. "That's a bit bourgeois, is it not?"

"Well, actually, it was me that bought it for him," she confessed.

Oh, Janey, dear Janey! Whatever will they say in the Partick steamie?

UNDER THE SKIN
OF AN ORANGEMAN

──────────── *13th July 1971* ────────────

Through the debris of a nightmare bombing raid on the centre of Belfast a few hours earlier, 40,000 Orangemen of Ulster and the world paraded to a pasture patch at The Finaghy Field yesterday to celebrate the Protestant victory of King William at the Battle of the Boyne in 1690.

In this land of poet and peat, of bombs and blarney, where the Mountains of Mourne sweep down to the sea and 11,000 British soldiers stand guard over their own people, the jaunty pilgrims engaged in their mid-summer march to add a touch of bitter irony to the current tragedy of North Ireland.

In the ranks of the Orange Order were visitors from Scotland and England, from Canada, and many other overseas countries.

Why do they come?

What is it that brings them to this cauldron of terror, to what many people believe is an inflammatory provocation to the minority Roman Catholic population?

While the Orange Order does not court publicity, individuals are not afraid to tell you why. Marching the seven miles there and back were men like 74-year-old George MacAdie, from Maryhill, Glasgow, who has been coming

151

to the Belfast parade since 1928.

Men like the Rev Ernest Linden-Ball, an Anglican priest from Norwich, who hasn't a Lodge nearby but who prides himself in his membership of the Cross of St Patrick Lodge in Belfast.

Mr Linden-Ball said: "The tragedy of the Church of England today is the retreat from the faith. The people of England—yes, they include some of my fellow-clergymen—just don't understand what we stand for.

"These men in the parade are the most charitable men I have ever known and they are also among the most courageous. They have a conviction of faith and if they see it being attacked, as it is, they have a duty to protect it.

"We are against nobody. We are for the Throne and the Scriptures. I shall continue to come here irrespective of bombs and bullets."

George MacAdie postponed a cataract operation to ease his encroaching blindness in order to be in the Belfast march.

"Protestantism brings me here," he says proudly. "I am a keen churchman at home, but the churches are not being attended. The Orange Order is the only thing that is making a show for Protestantism."

George, who belongs to Glasgow Lodge No 78 and used to be a mill worker at Renfrew, went on: "I come to show our solidarity. This year I just came on my own on the chartered boat.

"The lodge I used to walk with seems to have gone out of existence, so I met in with another lodge and they accepted me into their ranks."

Teetotaller George enjoyed his picnic-lunch in the glorious weather and parried a question about his attitude about Roman Catholicism.

"I would not like to give an opinion on that," he said. "My daughter married a Catholic and became one herself—

but I still speak to her and it hasn't really made a lot of difference."

George, who sees that his Staffordshire bull terrier attends Orange demonstrations in Scotland, caught the boat for Glasgow last night in readiness for his eye operation.

"They said I wouldn't march this year. But I did—and I'll be back again next year."

The sun shone at Finaghy Field as Ulstermen reaffirmed their loyalty to Queen and Protestant Faith.

In this memorable Irish picnic, there were buns, bands, and beer, songs and speeches, prayers and politics.

But there was, in a dour declaration of intent by Ulster's Protestants, absolutely and positively and seemingly forever "NO SURRENDER".

WIVES WHO REALLY
KNOW THEIR PLACE

22nd July 1971

If Scotland's eligible ladies were secretly engrossed in self-appraisal yesterday, it was more than likely in response to the advertisement of widower Charlie Reid, who wants a wife.

For Charlie, a farm worker from Ellon, Aberdeenshire, was quite specific about his requirements.

"Good cook . . . fond of children . . . must be clean-living." In short, she must be house-trained.

No mention of love, but then, as I might be able to explain from our common background, the Charlie Reids of this life are men of matter-of-fact good sense who have an uncanny knack of getting their priorities right.

In rural Aberdeenshire, the very mention of love is an embarrassment. All right for lah-dee-dah creatures with suede shoes and yellow gloves but not for the men who toil on dour clay to plant their seeds, raise their crops and gather the harvest.

For them, living and loving are an inseparable cycle in which tender words are nothing but an uncomfortable intrusion.

The energies of love are not to be wasted on gab, in

accordance with the down-to-earth principle that there is a time and a place for everything.

Plainly enough, Charlie's matrimonial applicants had better give up any thoughts of Women's Lib.

Charlie Reid simply wants a wife. And the Aberdeenshire definition of a wife as I remember it, is a woman who so respects her husband that she is willing to get up at first light, trauchle on all day with pots and pans and pigs and poultry, feeding, scrubbing, polishing, and caring in the way that a wife should.

In other words—a woman who knows her place in life.

It is not a popular definition, I know, but the reality of it is that it works.

Without statistical evidence, but with a lot of personal recollection, I would guess there is a lot more matrimonial contentment and a lot less divorce in rural Aberdeenshire than in most parts of Britain today.

Though the dour chiels of Foggieloan or Auchnagatt may not talk about the delicacies of love, they have their own peculiar ways of expressing it.

Slowly, but surely, they make their revelation—and the surprise of it is it has a habit of showing up as a sign of fulfilment on the faces of their womenfolk.

Life may be less of a bowl of cherries than a bowl of brose. But it does have its compensations!

MEN OF THE LAND

2nd September 1971

The claim of Scotland's farm workers for a basic wage of £18 a week brings into focus a breed of men whose worth is easily overlooked in an age of industrial congestion and free-for-all bargaining.

For my money they are the finest workers in Britain today. With a minimum of fuss, they go about an arduous job which is, in reality, more a way of life.

Following Nature's cycle from the ploughing of winter and seedtime of spring to the harvests of summer and autumn, they beat out the rhythms of the land as surely as they have carved their own special place in the social history of Scotland.

Who among us, with a memory that takes in the 1930s, can ever forget the feeing markets?

I still recall that exciting Wednesday at the end of May, and again at the end of November, when the farm servants flocked in to mingle with the farmers and to find themselves a six-month "fee".

When they had settled on an engagement, at perhaps no more than £10 or £12 for the half-year, the farmer would hand over the arles, which was a kind of binding luck-penny of a shilling, or half-a-crown if the farmer were generous.

Then the whole rustic business was bound up in a dram which was liable to develop into a continuing downpour.

Drunk men would roll in gutters or chase tormenting children before heading to their new "farm toun", to a world of brose and brawn, of kail, kye and kitchen lasses.

For those going to work the horses, there used to be an initiation into the secrecy of the "horseman's word", a code which was said to coax an unwilling Clydesdale into feverish activity while, by way of a bonus extra, having a similarly devastating effect upon an unwilling kitchen lass!

So the day dragged on, from the 5am start of feeding the horses, through two long "yokin's" and a "lowsing time" for lunch, to a supper-hour of 6.30, into an evening in which the squeeze-box or the haystack provided the basis of entertainment and a rough chaff-bed gave a lumpy, but well-earned rest.

But there is another memory of the feeing markets of Scotland which brought an excitement to our sleepy village scene.

No sooner had the gathering of farm folk begun than the pipes and drums of the Gordon Highlanders came swinging round the corner in full regimental dress, with more than music on their minds.

From ancient times, it had been part of the terms of lease that a farmer had to provide the soldiers of battle for the lairds of Scotland. Thus the armies of the 1715 and 1745 Rebellions were composed largely of farm servants—and the tradition did not die.

Up to the Second World War, recruiting sergeants appeared in the wake of the pipes and drums to gather up the men who could be diverted from their rural pursuits.

Many a lad who set out to find a farm "fee" and encountered John Barleycorn on the way, wakened up next morning to find himself committed to a life on the barrack-square.

The men of the land proved first-class soldiers. Not only were they strong and resilient but they were less likely to complain about cheerless billets, having come straight from chaumers which were generally at the wrong end of the luxury scale.

These men who till the soil and reap the corn, who ride their mechanical horses and add new skills to the crafts of husbandry which they take for granted, are of a breed and quality which remains peerless across the industrial front of Britain today.

If they have been more restrained in their demands for money, it is perhaps because they generally possess a depth of satisfaction and contentment—and wisdom—which seems to elude so many of us in a so-called enlightened society.

BOMBER TACTICS

Eric Brown, one-time railway fireman who became one of Scotland's most successful golfers, slept till after six last night, then bounded out of bed to pour me a whisky and to prove that the tiring journey back from America had done little to remove the sting from our Ryder Cup captain.

The British team had flown into Prestwick after putting up a best-ever performance on American soil. Brown was justifiably proud of the fact that the headlines had been captured by Scotsmen Harry Bannerman and Bernard Gallacher.

"The result was touch and go until near the end," he said, rubbing sleep from his eyes. "But with young lads like the ones I had in America we really have something to look forward to in two years time when they come over here.

"Yes, I had to tell our boys to be bombastic. I had to say 'These Americans are no better than you. Go out there and kill them.' The Americans, of course, had been on the golfing ascendancy since the 1930s and we still have a lot to do to turn the tide. But the gap is closing quickly.

"They have the advantages that they can play golf virtually all the year round and that their facilities are so much better.

We haven't spent a 100th part as much on sport as they have done.

"In fact, I believe it is time that Britain stopped bolstering countries which keep stabbing us in the back and spent more on sport. It would give the long-haired yobos more of a chance to participate.

"It is true that we have not produced the superstars of the calibre of the Americans but I believe that is changing. Tony Jacklin was coming into that category but unfortunately his game has deteriorated this year, probably because of his commitments outside tournament golf, having to play in exhibition games and so on.

"And we have others coming into the superstar class. Bernard Gallacher has the world at his feet and if Harry Bannerman can maintain the standard he showed in America then he, too, will be right up in that top class.

"And we have so many more, like Ronnie Shade, who is as good as any, Brian Barnes, who has opted for Scottish nationality, David Huish, Frank Rennie, David Ingram and so on—ach, we have the best bunch of Scottish professionals we have ever had."

Is golf really as clean a game as one would gather from the image of St Andrews, with all its sedate respectability? What about the Americans and their gamesmanship, which caused Harry Bannerman to wade in with good Scottish frankness during the Ryder Cup match?

"Oh, some of these Americans employ dubious tactics," says Brown, looking tanned and quite resplendent in his dressing gown.

"They don't allow their clubs to speak for them. They put it over as nervous traits, but it is funny how these things always seem to happen at a crucial point when we are about to make a stroke. I have had to put up with a lot of this kind of thing myself.

"The Americans are treated like prima donnas. They act like them—and they don't even endear themselves to their own people. I can tell you, in the Ryder Cup we had as many spectators on our side as they had on theirs.

"I don't have to engender hate in our lads. They know the score. For myself, I don't dislike the Americans off the course. It is true there are some I like better than others, such as Nicklaus, Trevino, Barber, Casper and Littler. They are the best of the American bunch. Now that we are home? Well, this must give the game in Scotland a tremendous boost."

Eric Brown, at 46 regarded as past his best, is still chasing that Open Championship title which has been within his grasp on four occasions.

He is a blunt, humorous, delightful character, proud of his two children and grateful to an understanding wife who has always been solemnly behind his golfing efforts.

This son of a former Bathgate school teacher, whose mother used to take him round the course when he was no more than four, is just the sort of chap we need to instil some determination into our international sportsmen.

For too long we have played the shrinking violets of world sport, applauding opponents when we should have been out there fighting.

With the Brown Bomber in charge there is no room for jolly old failures. And that, I guess, is not the worst attitude in the modern world.

END OF A CELTIC ERA—
SIR ROBERT'S 40 GREAT YEARS

—————————*22nd September 1971*—————————

The death of Sir Robert Kelly, so deeply regretted throughout the football world, brings to an end an incredible father-and-son succession which covers the entire 83-year history of Celtic Football Club.

For Sir Robert's father, James Kelly, was the club's first captain in 1888, later to become chairman. And Sir Robert, who was a few weeks short of his 69th birthday, joined the Celtic board in 1930 and became chairman in 1947.

On his resigning from the chair earlier this year, he was appointed president of the Celtic club.

So the family imprint was all over this famous institution from its beginnings as a means of raising money to provide soup kitchens for the poor of Glasgow's East End.

The triumph of leading Celtic to the pinnacle of European and world football in his latter years was fitting reward for a man who gave himself unsparingly to the ideals which guided his life.

High principles ensured that nothing cheap or flamboyant intruded on his success.

Bob Kelly—that was what he was until his knighthood two years ago—was a stockbroker by profession. He knew the benefits and disadvantages of being a lonesome man. He was difficult to know, introverted and sensitive and carrying a hint of the mystical in his make-up.

But he was always positive. Relentlessly he pursued his objectives with determination, irrespective of whatever brickbats that might bring.

There was something visionary in his view of the game of football, with its interdependence of club, player and spectator. He sensed dangers and opportunities alike and did not hesitate to give due warning of them.

He was the man who pioneered a youth policy at Celtic Park and then in 1965, having sensed the greatness of Jock Stein, called upon him to become boss of all things relating to the Celtic team.

He was the man who courageously spoke out against "the illegal and treacherous invasion of Czechoslovakia" by Russia, Poland, Hungary and East Germany in 1968 and declared himself ready to pull Celtic out of that year's European Cup competition.

The outcome was that the European authorities redrew the contest, excluding the invading countries.

From 1939 he had been in football legislation, becoming president of the Scottish League in 1950, president of the S.F.A. in 1960 and Scotland's representative on the European and world ruling bodies.

But he did not hesitate to resign from the Scottish Referee Committee when that body suspended referee Jim Callaghan last October in what Sir Robert considered a rank injustice.

He stood firm on Celtic's right to fly the flag of Eire at Celtic Park, declaring that he was merely keeping faith with the Irishmen who founded the club.

At all times he believed in discipline. In November, 1967, he was sickened by the treatment meted out to his players when they played for the unofficial club championship of the world in South America.

But he ruled that those who wear the Celtic jerseys should be above becoming involved in such a fracas and some of them had yielded to the temptation.

I'll never forget that day, when after his return to Glasgow, he drove up to Celtic Park in a taxi and, at a hastily convened Press conference, announced that he was fining each of his players £250.

One of Sir Robert's last pieces of advice to football followed the European Cup final in May of last year, when Celtic met Feyenoord of Rotterdam in Milan.

He considered it ridiculous that two teams from one corner of Europe should have to travel to another corner for the Final.

His suggestion, which might yet be taken up, is that two venues should be chosen in advance and the choice left until the finalists are known. Football matches, he said, are often arranged at short notice, and he could see no difference here.

In the days of his last illness, he struggled bravely to write his book, *Celtic*, which appeared last month as a unique contribution to a great story.

Sir Robert's brother Frank played for Celtic and three other brothers played for Queen's Park. But he himself never went beyond Junior grade, on the advice of his father.

For Robert had a deformed right arm and James Kelly told his son it was not only for his own sake but in fairness to his opponents that he should go no further in football.

The deep disappointment that he could never play for Celtic almost certainly sublimated a burning desire which in time arose in another form to play an even greater part in the destiny of the club.

Despite that deformity, he was winning tennis championships in his earlier years, holding racket and balls in one hand.

In 1969 he was knighted by the Queen at the Palace of Holyroodhouse, the first Scottish clubman to be so honoured. The bright, blue eyes sparkled with pride that day. And rightly so.

For Scotland had a wise and just administrator in her midst, a man of character. And his loss will be deeply felt.

Sir Robert, who lived in Burnside, Rutherglen is survived by his wife. There are no children.

Right on my own doorstep, a gas explosion at a new block of shops brought devastation to the Clarkston district, on the south side of Glasgow. Twenty people were killed.

CLARKSTON'S LAST TRIBUTE

When 2,000 Were United in a Day of Grief

——————————*30th October 1971*——————————

The sloping shafts of autumn brightness played down upon the many faces of tragedy in Clarkston's Greenbank Church yesterday when they gathered for the memory of those who died in last Thursday's disaster.

Half an hour before the service the people had filled the church and spilled to an overflow hall, bringing the total to close on 2,000.

They came in their many shades of involvement—the anonymous mass of those who were shop assistants, customers, rescue workers, neighbours, nurses—telling their own muted stories on grief-lined faces.

Scots Secretary Mr Gordon Campbell had come along, as had Viscount Muirshiel, Lord Lieutenant of Renfrewshire; Dr James Macfarlane, the county convener; Sir Donald Liddle, Lord Provost of Glasgow; Miss Betty Harvie Anderson, the local M.P.; Mr Ronald Parker, chairman of the Scottish Gas Board, and so on.

And they mixed with people like Catherine Proctor, the 18-year-old window dresser at Hamish Robertson's, who escaped the tragedy with nothing worse than shock; people like Archie Wright, whose shop in the disaster block survived, and who has since suffered the wrecking hand of vandals in his other shop in town.

They came in a common bond, expressed by the Rev Stanley Mair, of neighbouring Netherlee, when he quoted John Donne:

> "No man is an island, entire of itself;
> Any man's death diminishes me because I am
>   involved in Mankind;
> And therefore, never send to know for whom the bell tolls;
> It tolls for thee."

And they raised their voices in praise—it was broadcast to the nation—till the high notes were sometimes hard to strike.

The minister of Greenbank, the Rev Dr Angus Stewart, welcomed those of all faiths and none, and the lessons were read by Father Hearty of St Joseph's Roman Catholic Church and the Rev Colin Harrison, of St Aidan's Episcopal, Clarkston.

Dr Macfarlane came forward to tell of the messages of sympathy—none had touched him more than that of the people of Aberfan, who were remembering their own fifth anniversary when the demolition of Clarkston's shops erupted —and to express his thanks to the legion of unsung heroes who had worked so tirelessly in the name of rescue in the rubble that left 20 dead.

In his sermon, Mr Mair spoke of the sheer ordinariness of the disaster's context.

"It had been a most ordinary, peaceful scene of people serving and being served, people going home in buses or taking an afternoon walk—when suddenly it was tragedy.

"We are not going to try to answer the question 'Why?' because there is no answer in words. God gives an answer to those who are looking for it, through Jesus Christ who once hung on the Cross and who said 'My God, why hast

Thou forsaken Me?'

"We are not promised to be saved from trouble. We are promised to be saved in trouble. After the night there will be a morning.

"Death cannot separate us from the love of God—but what about life? Have we learned our lesson?

"How quickly we sometimes come to see other people as bothers instead of brothers. We start judging people according to ideas of status, separating ourselves according to our opinions, political, religious, social.

"Life will separate us again if we have not learned our lesson. Life must not be allowed to separate us from one another. For we are involved together and belong to one another."

With a resounding message of faith and compassion in their ears the people who had come together as Protestants, Catholics, Jews—of all faiths or none, as the minister said— went out to the afternoon sunshine in a spirit of friendliness that seldom pervades our daily contacts.

MY BOY TOMMY . . . MA DOC

I had a word with The Doc yesterday—a warm and wiry character whose world is football and who wears remarkably well at the age of 72. To complete the confusion, I might add that her Christian name is Georgina.

And, to clarify all, I should explain that the man who takes over this week as the saviour of Scotland's international football reputation is not the first of the Docherty dynasty to hold the abbreviated title.

That privilege fell to Ma Docherty, the widow woman who cleaned schools and tramped the streets as lamp-lighter to provide food for the boy who would one day gain fame as Scottish international footballer, captain and finally as the supremo to head us in the direction of the World Cup contest of 1974.

"Tommy tells you straight—just the same as masel'," says Georgina Docherty, who still lives in the same Glasgow east-side tenement in which she reared her three children back in the thirties.

"Whenever they used tae need a spokesman, they called for The Doc—that was me—and I used tae tell them!

"In those early days I was out workin' as cleaner and lamp-

169

lighter, makin' £4 odds a week. It was a struggle and the kids had to look after themselves—but it was a lively household.

"Tommy went tae work as a bakery van-boy and a' the time his heart was in football. One year he was goin' off tae the Isle of Man for a holiday but his call-up papers came and he never got.

"Instead, he was awa tae the Army in Palestine—ay, he became a sergeant in the H.L.I.—and I think that's where he got his domineering way. Mind you, playing football in the Army brought him out. I'm sure of that.

"His captain was Dr Adam Little o' the Rangers. One day, Tommy had come in and handed me £5 and said he got it for signing for Shettleston Juniors.

"I said: 'Awa and tak' it back.' But he said: 'I cannae. I've signed professional.' And I said: 'Well, ye shouldnae have. Ye should have signed amateur.' But it was too late.

"After a while with Celtic, he said: 'I'll never get my place at Parkhead with Bobby Evans there, so I'll take the first chance to leave.' And he went to Preston North End and then Arsenal and Chelsea.

"Now he is coming back tae Scotland and, honest, I never dreamed he would go this high.

"His wife comes from Girvan but of course his children have been brought up in England and have a bit o' that English tongue.

"Tommy has never really changed as a person. He is a determined man, with no airs or graces and he never forgets his friends. He is always crackin' jokes—in fact, I used to think he was going to be a comedian instead o' a footballer.

"When he comes home here now he takes me out in his Jaguar and drives me to East Kilbride or somewhere for lunch and he says 'Would ye no' like a car, Ma?' And I say 'Och, there's nothin' I'd like better, son, but I couldnae drive the bloomin' thing.'

"Some folk say Tommy is tough but it was just the way he played. He was great for thon slidin' tackles, wasn't he?" she enthuses.

But this is just the prelude to an interesting story of many years back which casts a revealing light on the true character of her famous son.

Georgina Docherty came home tired one night to find a little stranger asleep in the bed. Already without a mother, his father had been evicted and the boy had been found sleeping in an air raid shelter.

"Tommy said: 'Ma, we cannae leave the wee sowl sleepin' out in that damp shelter.' And he had brought him up and bathed him and wrapped one o' his own shirts round him and put him tae bed.

"And he helped me to care for that boy, who stayed with us for the next 10 years until he could go off on his own."

It is the kind of story which needs to be remembered when we assess the man who has breathed new life into Scottish football. Tough, demanding, uncompromising? All of them.

But also a man who cares—about football, about Scotland, about people who are prepared to give of their best.

Is it really such a bad basis for the job to which he now applies himself with such vigour?

SALT OF THE EARTH—THOSE MEN
WHO FACE THE SEA

—————————*27th January 1972*—————————

The men who go down to the sea in little ships seldom pause to count the cost. It is a passion of their blood, a course to be followed without question.

They fish to live—and live to fish.

And when the great storms come swelling out of the unknown and toss them to the mercies of watery mountains, that too is accepted as their particular way of life.

In the North-East port of Fraserburgh and neighbouring villages the prayers for safety recede in their hopefulness if not their strength.

More than two weeks now have passed since the men of the local fishing boat *Nautilus* were last reported 85 miles north-east of Lerwick in the Shetlands.

Since then, only the silence that stirs fear in the hearts of every woman who waves her man goodbye as he heads for the wide open spaces of the ocean.

There is very little chance that Stephen McNab and his brother-in-law Ian Tait and uncle William Stephen and the others can still be alive.

The skipper is a safety-conscious man who took part in the roll-call method of keeping in touch with other vessels.

172

But no amount of thought and care will help when the massive waves off the Scottish coast mark out a victim.

Stephen McNab was only 30, the father of two boys. He comes from an extraordinary little village called Cairnbulg (it is joined to the twin village of Inverallochy) which lies round the bay from Fraserburgh.

The local pronunciation is "Cyarnbulg" and the inhabitants are known as "Bulgers". In Fraserburgh they joke about going "ower the watter", which means nothing more adventurous than travelling round to Cairnbulg.

Within its irregular little streets it contains a particularly worthy breed of seafaring men, duplicated in other nearby communities like St Combs and Sandhaven and Rosehearty.

The weather-beaten faces are creased with character, solid human beings with a searching honesty which makes them both compassionate and critical—and as reliable as the beam of Fraserburgh lighthouse.

I was there two years ago when the Fraserburgh lifeboat went down with five lives. By coincidence, I had been there as a young reporter when the lifeboat turned turtle in the previous disaster of 1953.

And I found an unchanging breed of people, showing the same kind of courage which seems to favour the people of the sea. It had been there in 1919 when Fraserburgh lost yet another lifeboat.

It was there during the war when the town took a pasting, particularly on the night when German bombers were drawn by a spectacular fire in the local Benzie and Miller's shop.

"These people realise that danger is part of their lives in a fishing community," says the Rev A. A. S. Mitchell, who has conducted memorial services for two local lifeboat crews.

"The women are still clinging to a lingering hope over the *Nautilus*, but they realise that it is slender. I think we shall be holding a special service on Sunday . . ."

173

And there, perhaps, we come to the heart of the matter. You cannot consider the life of our fishermen without mention of their faith. They may follow a large variety of routes, from Auld Kirk and Baptist to Close Brethren and Pentecostal, but they arrive at the same belief in a life for which the present one is only a preparation.

Duration, therefore, becomes a matter of less importance than quality. And nobody can fault them on that score.

For they are the salt of the earth, these men who go out to face the perils of the sea, surpassed only by the women-folk who wait and worry and quietly pray—and finally accept whatever fate the good Lord may have in store.

WAS IT REALLY A LOVE AFFAIR?

For more than a century now the rumours and arguments have raged about the association of Queen Victoria and her manservant John Brown. Magazines of her day went as far as to report that they were secretly married and that she had gone abroad to have Brown's baby.

The reports were nonsense, but Victoria's own reaction to the baby story was merely to laugh. She was, to say the least of it, indiscreet in her connection with Brown and, according to the American author, Elizabeth Byrd, she was almost certainly in love with him.

Miss Byrd was, in fact, putting the finishing touches to her latest historical novel, *The Long Enchantment*, when I dropped in at her flat overlooking the Palace of Holyrood in Edinburgh this week.

Miss Byrd, who came to live in Scotland after writing her best-selling novel on Mary Queen of Scots, *Immortal Queen*, absorbed her information and atmosphere while actually living at Crathie, near Balmoral, where John Brown's father was schoolmaster.

The basic facts are that the teenage Brown, who was eight years younger than the Queen, was a stableman at Balmoral

175

before she bought it. He became a ghillie and a great favourite of Prince Albert, who asked him to lead the Queen's pony when they went on their safaris into the hills.

John Brown was a tall, good-looking, red-bearded man with hypnotic eyes, according to all accounts, and Victoria herself was very fond of him. But there was nothing untoward in their relationship until after Albert's death in 1861, when the Queen was in her early 40s.

"She appointed him her personal attendant, on constant call, and gradually it became much more intimate," says Miss Byrd.

"When she went to pieces and began the long mourning, Brown had to lift her from couch to bed and back again; he was in and out of her room without knocking and could sit down in her presence and smoke and even drink if he liked—and he did. He was a heavy drinker and taught the Queen to drink whisky.

"My novel doesn't leave Balmoral but Brown did in fact accompany the Queen everywhere, including tours abroad, becoming devoted and protecting her from all that bored her, including her own family and Prime Minster Gladstone, whom she never liked.

"One evening at Balmoral, Brown, who was honest, sincere but very blunt, was standing behind the Queen at dinner as Gladstone was going on and on about something.

"He could see that she was bored and that he had to take some kind of action. So he tapped their Prime Minister on the shoulder and said sternly 'That's enough, that's enough!'—and Gladstone had to shut up."

But what is the actual evidence of Queen Victoria's love for John Brown? I wondered.

"When a woman loves a man," Miss Byrd began with a mellow look and an authoritative tone, "she can't stop talking about him. And she talks about him a great deal in her leaves.

"When Brown died at Windsor in 1883, aged 56, nobody could bring himself to tell her. The shock paralysed her legs and for days she would not see anyone or put her signature to anything.

"She even wanted to write a biography of John Brown but was finally dissuaded by the Dean of Windsor. She also wanted to publish his diary but was persuaded to have it destroyed."

Was the affair ever sexually consummated?

"I wouldn't dream of saying Yes or No. Though she was prim, prudish and pious she was also a very passionate woman sexually—it is said that she wore out poor Albert, who hated his role as royal stud—but whether she actually went to bed with Brown nobody will ever know.

"Her son Bertie—later King Edward VII—loathed Brown because he was so blunt with him. One day he came into Balmoral demanding to see his mother. Brown said she was having a nap, and when the future king insisted he was told in no uncertain manner to go off and amuse himself!

"After Victoria's death, Bertie destroyed almost every statue and cairn which the Queen had raised for John. But he did not dare tamper with the loving inscription which she had placed on his gravestone at Crathie Churchyard."

But Queen Victoria seems to emerge as more of a red-blooded being than her stony portraits suggest. She used to appal titled ladies by encouraging the tradition of the ghillies' balls at Balmoral, where they had to dance with "uncouth, sweaty, drunken servants."

It is a measure of the lady who reigned for those sixty glorious years that such earthy experiences did nothing to blunt the feminine appetites which evidently burned so fiercely beneath those skirted folds.

DAME SYBIL STOLE THE SHOW

———————————29th February 1972———————————

Dame Sybil Thorndike, that Grand Old Lady of the Theatre who will be 90 in October, is still reeling with excitement about one of her greatest-ever nights of acclamation.

At her home in Swan Court, Chelsea, yesterday she took time off from her music, her reading and writing to tell me:

"I went along expecting a rather ordinary affair, to be opening an envelope and announcing the best film of the year. And suddenly the whole of the Albert Hall rose to its feet.

"I was surprised and thrilled. It must have been because I am so old!"

It was much more than that, Dame Sybil. And, for the millions watching the annual presentation of awards for television and the cinema, it was one of the most significant moments ever produced on the small screen.

Out of the backcloth she came, fresh and beautiful, smiling and waving her stick to a vast audience. Quickly, the significance of the occasion spread itself around and, with fine spontaneity, the gathering began to rise to its feet.

After the presentation to the director of the top film, Dame Sybil wandered across unrehearsedly to talk to the Princess

178

and the cameras gave us a magnificent view of their totally uninhibited conversation.

"It was a great thrill to speak to Princess Alexandra," Dame Sybil told me. "I am still well and strong but I am in pain all the time with arthritis."

Well, it didn't show at the Albert Hall. It was a face lit up with uncamouflaged pleasure.

A thousand thanks, Dame Sybil—we loved you!

BACK THROUGH THE YEARS
WITH BOOTHBY

———————— *11th March 1972* ————————

Baron Boothby of Buchan and Rattray Head sat silver-haired in his London flat this week reviewing the past, present and the future.

He spanned through the 35 years he was the rugged, individualistic Tory member for Aberdeenshire East, a career which earned him the titles ... Rebel ... and the Gay Cavalier of British politics!

Bubbling with all his old verve the 72-year-old baron, who today sits as an Independent Member of the Lords, was frank about Scotland, about Churchill, about his own crisis and not least, about the present Government.

As a Tory who was noted for his shrewd judgements and accurate forecasts, he told me:

"In all my political life I have never seen a situation so badly handled by any Government as the miners' strike. They thought they could beat the miners as they had beaten the postal workers but they under-estimated their strength and determination.

"The miners would have settled for terms which were reasonable and well-deserved before the strike even started if only the Government had intervened in time. It was

180

obvious that the Government was going to be beaten.

"Now they give the impression of being in disarray—of being on the run. The Prime Minister has great qualities of integrity and determination—he's like steel—but he is not a warm character and in that position you do need warmth. Lloyd-George had it. Churchill had it up to a point. But who are the Government's men today? Davies?—No. Carr?—No. Whitelaw?—a disappointment. I'd say Carrington is the best of the bunch.

"I don't see them on the other side either. Harold Wilson is a close friend but he has not played his cards at all well and he has damaged his credibility over Europe.

"We are lacking the personalities in politics. They are going into industry and commerce now, those men like Maxwell Joseph.

"The old Clyde group of M.P.s served a very useful purpose in the Commons by expressing Scotland. But where are the Wheatleys, the Maxtons, the Kirkwoods, the Geordie Buchanans?"

Lord Boothby, whose father, a director of the Bank of Scotland, wrote that famous love song *Jean, Jean, my Bonnie, Bonnie Jean*, has long declared his philosophy as one of scepticism, tolerance and invincible optimism. Did I detect a shading off in the latter?

"A sense of humour has carried me through life but there is perhaps a little more pessimism in me. The First World War, you see, destroyed a generation but the Second World War destroyed Western civilisation as we knew it.

"Values have gone and they are not being replaced. The British Empire, which was a stabilising force despite what people said about it, has also gone and that is a tragedy.

"I still stick to what I once said, that the English would be sunk without the Scots. We are undoubtedly the sanest, nicest and most generous people in the world, with a marvellous capacity for integrating. Politically, we are extraordinarily sane.

"But I am concerned about Scotland industrially. The farmers and fishermen will be all right—I like to think that the 12-mile fishing limit which sparked off so much prosperity was one of my achievements in life—but there are far too many disputes along the Central Belt.

"The car strikes are extremely damaging. I don't know what has gone wrong with the workers in the Central Belt but something is biting them."

Was it not a source of great disappointment that his widely-acknowledged talents landed him, not in the heights of statemanship but on the less elevated levels of television entertainment?

"I could never have remained in Government for any length of time," he boomed. "I would have been too strongly opposed, for example, to appeasement over Hitler and to the Suez invasion. Being a rebel comes naturally to me. I was a Radical Tory in the tradition of Joseph Chamberlain."

Having been groomed for political stardom in the shadow of Churchill, what about the rift which eventually came?

"At first we worked well together over questions like rearming. I had gone to Germany in 1934 and was summoned to see Hitler at the Embassy Hotel.

"I went fortified with a good lunch, and when I had walked along the corridor, which was there to intimidate, there he was sitting in his brown shirt and swastika.

"He rose, clicked his heels, raised his right arm and said 'Hitler!' The lunchtime hock came mercifully to my rescue and, with great style, I clicked my heels, raised my right arm and said 'Boothby!'

"When I was called to see Chamberlain, I told him that we were dealing with a madman with a destructive genius without parallel and that he had better realise it. Chamberlain said 'I am sorry, I don't agree.'

"As for Churchill, he gave me office when he became Prime Minister but there was a row between us. I wrote to tell him how to run the war and he didn't like it. Nobody more than I admired his conduct in 1940 but he was a tyrant in power and became more and more dictatorial and difficult to serve.

"I was doing good work at the Ministry of Food but he was critical of me and friction grew between us."

Then came the 1941 crisis in Boothby's personal life, when he supported the move to freeze Czechoslovakian assets in this country, to be paid out to those who had lost money when Hitler invaded that country.

He was chastised for not declaring a personal interest.

"After the war, Churchill picked me to go to the Council of Europe, where I spent seven years. Then he gave me the K.B.E. and that put paid to any suggestion of misconduct. You don't make a crook into a Knight of the Order of the British Empire, and that was a boost to my prestige."

A LESSON IN COUNTING
YOUR BLESSINGS . . .

―――――――――― *10th April 1972* ――――――――

DATELINE: LOURDES
The broken bodies of young Scots children were dipped in the water of Lourdes today—and a fresh glow of warmth came shining from their faces.

In the massive Rosary Square, with its grey tiered basilicas, the harmony of 10,000 voices soared through the trees, a unison of sound and spirit that will linger in the memory forever.

The Scots have come to the South of France with the Handicapped Children's Pilgrimage Trust.

Lourdes is a lesson on how to count your blessings. For here the sick of all nationalities come trekking in a continuous procession, to pray at that niche in the rock where the Virgin Mary appeared to a 14-year-old girl called Bernadette Soubirous in 1858.

She asked for a chapel to be built there and for people to come in processions. She guided Bernadette to a spot by the grotto at which she was to scrape the earth for a spring of water. It began to flow—and the Water of Lourdes has been flowing ever since at the rate of 27,000 gallons a day.

A local blind man bathed his eyes that first night and his

sight returned. Since then thousands of cures have been claimed, but the Vatican's medical team has acknowledged only 70 as being beyond any other explanation.

Thus it was that a small French town became a shrine for all the world to visit.

Thus it was that Tom Connelly, a time-study engineer from Dundee and chairman of the Handicapped Children's Pilgrimage Trust in Scotland, brought 67 Scottish children and almost as many helpers to Lourdes.

There are 650 British children here this week with the Trust, started 18 years ago by Dr Michael Strode from Sussex. Expenses are largely met by people who donate their trading stamps and it costs the children nothing.

Tom Connelly had not given much thought to the handicapped until his own son became disabled after hitting his head in a fall. The boy has a chance of a cure.

But Tom now devotes much of his spare time to the welfare of those who haven't. So he organised the Scottish party for Lourdes and roped in an amazing cross-section of assistants.

Maire Docherty, from Merrylee, Glasgow, works in a Govan insurance office and acts as Scottish secretary. Along came three nurses from the Princess Margaret Rose Hospital in Edinburgh—Kathleen Melloy, of Edinburgh, Helen Gaughan, from Rosyth, and Anna McCleary, from Luton.

They were joined by people like Moyra Fitzgerald, from Kent—she is a niece of *Daily Express* racing tipster Scotia—and Winifred Mallon, former general secretary of the Royal College of Obstetricians and Gynaecologists.

They needed some able-bodied men, so Tom cajoled two of his acquaintances from Dundee to come along—Arthur Jones, a car salesman, and Joe Smith, a packaging salesman.

Father John Connelly, from Aberdour, Fife, is here, along with his brother, Father Tom Connelly, from Dover, and his two sisters, Mary and Kitty. They are cousins of chairman

Tom. Father Joe Connelly, from Cranhill, Glasgow, their uncle, is also here.

The helpers have paid their own way in this service to the sick. Their reward is the joy which shows already in these children, most of whom are away from their parents for the first time.

There are children like Billy Abel (13) from Dundee, Kenneth Gardner (15) from Hamilton, and Simon Blasbury (11), Dundee, all spastics; John Paul (14) from Edinburgh, who has spent years in hospital with hip joint trouble; Albert Black (11), Dundee, with muscular dystrophy; Gerald Kane (13) Hamilton, with a pancreas ailment.

There are Catherine Young (12) from Edinburgh, an asthmatic, Tessa Raeburn from Dr Barnardo's Home, Wishaw, an orphan with a heart condition, and two East Kilbride youngsters, Louise Murphy (15), an epileptic, and Brian Maher (16), who is deaf.

You don't have to be a Roman Catholic or even a believer at all to know that the sick are feeling the better for it. They have come without idle dreams of miracles and they leave refreshed. The miracle is more of spirit than body.

Ten-year-old Ann MacDonald from Motherwell, one of the thalidomide tragedies of the sixties, beams widely as she tells me: "Oh I'm having a lovely time."

And she has a rival in another 10-year-old, Calum McIntyre, a spina bifida case from Rothesay, who says: "What I like best here is the statue of Our Lady at the Grotto."

Says Ann: "I liked when the priest came to bless us."

Both are Celtic supporters. And when I asked Calum if he had ever been abroad before, his smile widened as he said: "Ay, I've been to Glasgow!"

And so it went on—mirth without moans. Then it was time to go to the birthday party for three of the Scots children—Ann Gallagher (10) from Easterhouse, Desmond

Docherty (14) from Uddingston, and John McCafferty (16) from Newarthill, Lanarkshire.

Down in Rosary Square they still came flocking to the candlelight procession, those with eyes that cannot see, limbs that cannot move, lives that have little expectation.

For the rest of my life, I shall remember them singing the haunting refrain of the Ave Maria. And I shall remember little Ann MacDonald as she sang at that birthday party a jaunty melody of a different type—"Singing in the Rain."

NO MEAN WELCOME
IN NO MEAN CITY

——————— *7th July 1972* ———————

Her Majesty the Queen drove down the Old Rutherglen Road of Glasgow yesterday and virtually put the royal seal of destruction on the Gorbals that was.

It was there, on that very street, that the fictitious Johnny Stark and his mob of the '20s pursued their gangsterish feuds of "No Mean City" amid the tomcat stenches of the slums and the depressing atmosphere of the time.

It was then that they generated a warmth and rugged friendliness and neighbourliness that gave a flavour and comfort to their living.

But the bleak congestion had to go. They razed the old Gorbals to the ground during the '60s and put up their fine new blocks of flats, complete with bathrooms.

After giving the send-off to yet another development yesterday, the Queen and Prince Philip walked freely among the people in the neighbouring Queen Elizabeth Square, which she had opened in 1961.

It was a day of uninhibited Gorbals joy—the flags, the cheers, the informal chats and laughter and the sunshine, which toothless women would fain have credited to the radiance of the Queen!

Her Majesty looked up again at the huge block of flats which bears her name and waved to the people above.

Few people would call that particular building their favourite piece of architecture—and I doubt if anyone had the nerve to tell her that it is now commonly known on the south side of Glasgow as Alcatraz, such are the prison-like corridors and feeling of confinement.

It is the price of progress. Women who were once condemned to the warrens of Florence Street and Mathieson Street and Camden Street were in nostalgic mood as Her Majesty drove into Cumberland Street.

"Ach, I'd raither be back in Mathieson Street ony day," said Mrs Mary Gray, who moved down the road to the new flats of Waddel Court. And her pal, Ann Lavery agreed.

"Your life's no' free," she said. "I'm up on the 17th flair and honest, ye feel like a prisoner. Wi' the kids on holiday it's murder. They can haud the lifts at the bottom and stop ye gettin' doon. The spirit o' the Gorbals has gone."

Miss Jessie McGowan, who grew up in the Gorbals, said: "We try to carry the spirit o' the old Gorbals into the new flats. When I was in hospital, a neighbour had my hoose papered when I got back. That's what used tae happen more often."

So they have taken whole streets of the Gorbals and turned them on their ends like rising matchboxes. They have enclosed them in their little high-rise compartments, like battery hens, cut off from the mateyness of the tenements.

But, given a chance, I suspect that the spirit of the people is little different.

PS: Nothing is for ever. That Queen Elizabeth block was dynamited to the ground in 1993!

IT'S ALL A GAME TO LEE

—————————— *11th July 1972* ——————————

The ballyhoo of anticipation built up at Muirfield yesterday for the arrival of that swarthy, talkative, colourful little Mexican from Texas, Lee Trevino, who was coming back to defend the British Open Golf Championship which he won last year.

But Lee was late. And any visions of a Rolls-Royce arrival were shattered in splendid fashion when the bouncing bundle of golfing genius—second in the world only to Jack Nicklaus—rolled up in a modern little automobile to reveal the funny story of what happened to him on the way to the Open.

"Where have you been, Lee?" they called, as he stepped out, complete with Mexican hat, to spread greetings and favours around the adoring horde.

"I've been on a tour of Scotland," came the reply. "Seen every wheatfield and tractor in the whole of this land of golf. I guess somebody somewhere got it messed up but Derick Pillage, my manager over here, had three limousines waiting for use at Edinburgh Airport. That was fine—except that I flew in to Prestwick.

"So I ended up with no transportation. Seven of us hired a bus but we had to stop so often for directions that one tractor passed us four times.

But the ebullient Lee arrived all right, fresh from Niagara Falls where he had come 10th in the Canadian Open at the weekend—actually he didn't know where he had finally finished until some golfing journalists put him right.

"When you have so much money as I have you don't worry any more," he joked.

"I am very conscious when coming to Scotland that I have come to the home of golf," he told me.

"There was a time when I thought you couldn't play in wind and rain and stuff like that. I thought the people over here must be crazy to go out in these conditions. But I don't think so any more. Gee I'd think there was something wrong if there was no wind and rain. I love it!

"I was real ill with pneumonia just a few weeks ago but I guess that helped me in some ways.

"As Jack Nicklaus was saying, it is often better to build up to an event like this—though I didn't exactly try to get pneumonia for that purpose!

"But I am seeing real well again. I haven't had a drink for nine weeks and honest, I didn't know the courses looked that good!"

SCOTS HONOUR A BATTLE HERO

8th September 1972

The treatment of Lord Dowding, the man who master-minded our heroic defence in the Battle of Britain, is still a matter for fierce argument whenever people get round to discussing the Second World War.

For Dowding, introvert, spiritualist and lonesome Air Chief Marshal in charge of Fighter Command, was not everybody's cup of tea.

He had made an enemy of Churchill for one thing.

But he stuck to his guns, led us to victory in the greatest air battle of the war and was "rewarded" by being the only successful commander who was NOT made a Marshal of the Royal Air Force after it was all over.

The treatment seemed shabby. Dowding was quietly retired and lived through another generation of neglect until he died in 1970, having at least seen himself vindicated by the film "Battle of Britain".

But, happily, it does not end there. Thanks to the single-handed efforts of a wartime WAAF from Scotland, a splendid memorial is to be unveiled tomorrow in the Dumfriesshire town of Moffat (population 2,000).

For it was there—and how many Scots would have

192

guessed it?—that Hugh Dowding was born and spent the first 15 years of his life.

It was there that Miss Irene Park, whose father was local doctor for 50 years, conceived the idea of a memorial.

And it is there this weekend that Lady Dowding and several of "The Few" will gather with local people for the unveiling ceremony and to hear Group Captain Douglas Bader deliver an address on the second half of the memorial—an appeal for £10,000 from the people of Britain to endow a bed at the R.A.F. Association Home at Sussexdown.

A Spitfire (the one which once took off with a WAAF sitting on the tail!) and a Hurricane from Bader's old squadron will fly past at 500ft and a trumpeter will sound the fanfare.

Miss Park, a gracious lady in middle-age, explained to me how it all came about.

"I happen to have the double interest of serving in the WAAF and of knowing about Lord Dowding's connection with my town," she said. "It seemed that nothing had been done in his memory anywhere else and you cannot push a thing like that upon people. I knew that there would always be an interest in a memorial in Moffat and that it would always be cared for here. Knowing of my double connection, there were so many people getting in touch with me about it that it almost became a pressure to do something. I took it up with the R.A.F. Association."

But how did the Dowding family come to be in Moffat in the first place?

"Hugh Dowding's father was, I understand, a master at Fettes School in Edinburgh but he decided to set up a preparatory school in Moffat—together with a gentleman called Mr Churchill!

"Lord Dowding was born here in 1882 and lived in Moffat until 1897. The school changed form after that but it is once more a prep school today. Among the former pupils of St Ninian's was the late Mr Iain Macleod, the Tory Minister.

"Lord Dowding became one of our earliest airmen, but he was back to visit Moffat in later years. There are still some older people who remember the family."

There, at the scene of his boyhood haunts, they have erected a fine sandstone memorial in the magnificent setting of Station Park (couldn't they now change that outmoded name to Dowding Park?).

A bronze plaque includes his portrait in bas-relief with simple words to express the nation's gratitude and a reminder that he was "Born in Moffat".

The motto of that happy little township in the Border hills is "Ever Aye Ready", as good a guide as any for the young Hugh Dowding as he went off to start a career in the air.

Apart from Lady Dowding and Douglas Bader, the guests tomorrow will include men like the Duke of Hamilton, Group Captains Gilroy and Denholm from Edinburgh, Air Vice Marshall Sandy Johnstone and other Battle of Britain pilots, including some of the Poles who joined in the epic.

Churchill's grandson, the young Winston, has sent his blessing for the event and the whole spirit of the occasion will be summarised in the immortal words of the warrior which are included on the memorial stone:

"Never in the field of human conflict was so much owed by so many to so few."

And a lone Spitfire will ring its own fanfare across a peaceful sky. Paradoxically, on this occasion at least, the prophet hath some honour in his own land.

BING: I WOULDN'T BE A HIT NOW

———————— *14th September 1972* ————————

We were talking about the legend of Bing Crosby and the man at the other side of the coffee pot was a leading witness to the subject—Bing himself, still incredibly active though his next birthday will take him into his 70th year.

Bing came quietly into Scotland, sooner than expected, for Friday's inauguration of a new golf tournament at St Andrews.

It is for the over-60's and the Old Groaner's generosity has ensured that there will be a Bing Crosby cup to compete for in the years to come.

But we left golf behind and looked at the life of the incredible Crosby, his fame and his fortune, touching briefly on topics life faith, hope and charity.

"Bob? Yes I hear from him. He calls me up whenever he has a new joke. I don't have too many calls really."

Most of the time, however, Bing was serious—and frank about himself. From a man whose velvet voice created new world records for disc sales, there was an admission:

"I don't sell many records any more. A few of the standards, like *White Christmas*, *Home on the Range* and *Don't Fence Me In*, still sell, but that's about it.

"A has-been? Well, things have changed since I was singing and I realise that my day is over. I am grateful for what has happened in the past and I am certainly not envious of anyone doing well now.

"I'm just kinda glad I came when I came. There wasn't so much competition then, only four or five people singing like I did. Now there are thousands.

"To be a success today, a singer has to be very good and very lucky. He has to hit upon a great song which will project him immediately and he has to capitalise on that development by expanding his repertoire, taking in every possible type of song.

"Apart from people like Sinatra, Andy Williams and Perry Como—I like to evaluate singers by their voice, personality and presence—the ones I like today include Petula Clark, Matt Munro and Tom Jones.

"Tom can sing anything in any range—if only he would stand still and not wiggle! Still, I suppose the young girls like it.

"Myself? I don't think I would have been a star today. I don't think I would even have got a job," he added with a modesty which was excessive but not false.

What about the Voice itself?

"It hasn't sung for three months. Occasionally I burst into song in the bath or for the kids, but I'm lazy and I don't sing enough to keep my vocal chords in trim."

After the death of his first wife, Dixie Lee, Bing married Kathryn Grant and they live, with their three children, just outside San Francisco.

From there, Bing measures out a working year which includes about 16 television shows, some guest spots and an assortment of appeal-type programmes which show that his name is still a persuasive force around America.

Recently he completed an album with Count Basie, the

only recording he has made for a number of years.

"But I love recording," he says with childlike enthusiasm. "It is perhaps the thing I do which brings me most enjoyment. I see the musicians I used to know and they work out little arrangements and we really have a picnic."

Sitting back in his chair Bing remembered his childhood: "There was always music about our home. Mother and father sang, my sister played the piano and we had the phonograph records.

"Whenever there was a parish entertainment, I was up there singing something but I had no thoughts of being a star. I just followed the popular singers of the day, like Al Jolson, and began to feel I wanted to be part of that life.

"The word 'crooner' had been applied to Rudi Vallee and the word came to cover those of us who sang in that soft manner. I guess my popularity was helped by the fact that audiences could relate to me. I looked like one of them. There was nothing artificial. I was like the boy round the corner who just happened to get lucky.

"I was also lucky in the people who were writing songs at that time, men like Jerome Kern, a man of charm and wit and a marvellous composer.

"And, of course, Irving Berlin, who wrote so many great tunes, including 'White Christmas'. What that song did for me was tremendous. He is still very active in his 80s. He phones me up from time to time."

Bing laughs off the talk of a fabulous Crosby fortune and undertakes to give it some serious calculation. Then he emerges with this deduction:

"If I were to reduce everything to cash, pay taxes on it and find that I was left with one-and-a-half million dollars, I'd be happy."

Crosby has come straight to Britain from the Olympic Games where he became well-known around the Village and deeply concerned about the tragedies surrounding it.

Does he see any hopeful signs in the distressing world about him?

"I see a trend towards religious attitudes," he says. "I'm not a professional Catholic—I don't make a song about my religion, because it is a very private thing—but a man must have faith.

"If a man expects to get the benefits from what we call civilisation, he must produce and he must be accountable."

And then this likeable, natural man—a legend in homely tweed jacket and little white hat—walked out into the sunshine of the Old Course.

URQUHART ON ARNHEM:
'A FAIR RISK, I WOULD DO IT AGAIN.'

———————— *22nd September 1972* ————————

Twenty-eight years ago this week, 1,500 soldiers died in the battle of Arnhem, another 6,000 were wounded or captured.

The Scots were there in force, from KOSBs to Paratroopers, and the whole British operation was led by that sturdy Scottish soldier, General Robert E. Urquhart who, aged 70, now lives quietly by the Port of Menteith, near Aberfoyle.

Yesterday I asked General Urquhart:

"If the battle were tomorrow, would you make any changes? Do you blame yourself? What are your feelings now when you pay your periodic private visits to Arnhem?"

He pondered the questions in the peace of his study above the Lake of Menteith and told me:

"Of course I feel sad about the number of men who were killed and I wish that certain things had turned out in a different way.

"It was an ambitious plan but it was a fair risk and I would do it again. Another time, I would hope that the airlift would go better. There was a shortage of planes, which meant that I could not expect to be at full strength for three days.

"Then there was the unexpected presence of two German

199

Panzer Divisions. Our men kept asking 'Where is the Second Army which is coming to join us?'

"I myself could have done better by staying at my headquarters instead of getting separated from it for 36 hours. But the wireless was not working and I went off to find out what was going on.

"The result was that I had to hide in a house, three or four miles away, with a German armoured vehicle just outside the door! When I was away decisions had to be taken by someone else.

"But we did have partial success. We denied the bridge to the Germans for four days and attracted a lot of attention by our resistance on the perimeter for five more days.

"Looking back, I would say that we did not make enough use of the local people. At first, we regarded them with some suspicion, not quite knowing who they would be supporting. But the Dutch were wonderful. To this day, they regard the battle as their own: it is a piece of their history and they have always given us tremendous hospitality."

This tall, courteous soldier was never bitter about the pasting he took at Arnhem.

He told me: "You have to take war as it comes, becoming very impersonal. They are just the enemy and you shoot, but don't call it murder. It is, after all, your job . . ."

SCOT WILLIE CARSON
TAKES PIGGOTT'S CROWN

—————————— *2nd November 1972* ——————————

Come Saturday afternoon at Haydock Park and the horse-racing world will officially acclaim a brave little man from Stirling who glows from the heart with Scottish pride.

For Willie Carson, fastest fly-weight on four legs, will become the champion jockey of Britain for 1972, wearing the crown which had practically taken up residence on the head of the peerless Piggott.

With 131 winners to his credit, the 29-year-old Scot cannot be beaten by Irishman Tony Murray.

So the incredibly slender No 1 jockey to Lord Derby and his trainer, Bernard Van Cutsem, will gather a few friends in Newmarket on Saturday night and hold a celebration.

Among those present will be his parents, Tommy and May Carson, who raised him first in a prefab and then around the corner in a council house at 92 Cornton Road, Stirling.

Mr Carson worked as warehouse foreman with Fyffe's bananas and his wife had a job at the Fourways Restaurant, Dunblane. Young Willie attended Riverside School.

"People kept saying that little Tich here would have to be a jockey, so I was kind of brainwashed into it," the new champion recalls as we chat in the spacious Newmarket house which Lord Derby keeps for his top jockey. That other great rider, Doug Smith, was the previous occupant.

"Through her job, my mother knew a Mrs McFarlane who had a riding school and I went there every week from the age of 10 until I left school at 15.

"I was then apprenticed to Gerald Armstrong at half-a-crown a week and was with Sam Armstrong at Newmarket before coming to Lord Derby and Mr Van Cutsem.

"Although Newmarket is the home of horse-racing because of its facilities, it is not a good centre from which to work. Of course you must live where your horses are but it takes me at least two hours to get to most racecourses.

"On a typical day, I'm out on the heath by about 7.30, coming back about nine by which time the phone has started ringing. Then it's off to the racecourse—my wife Carole often drives—or sometimes I charter a plane and fly to two meetings a day, perhaps not getting home until midnight.

"Weary? Ach, there's always something different happening. Certainly my appetite for racing is keener now than it was 10 years ago."

What about the other appetite, which most jockeys have to control so rigidly to keep their weight down?

"I don't have to diet much," says Carson, demonstrating his 7st 8lb frame. "I have tea and toast for breakfast, perhaps a few cups of tea during the day but, like all jockeys, my main meal is at night, when I can eat anything I want."

Willie Carson, who survived a serious car crash five years ago, modestly declares that good horses make good jockeys, but concedes that he has put in a lot of hard work to reach the top.

"I have had a bit of luck too—but oddly enough very little luck in Scotland. In my earlier days with Sam Armstrong I used to do quite well, but more recently I don't seem to get the right horses in Scotland. I come up once or twice a year, but they just don't go for me.

"It's a pity, because there is nothing I would like better than to do well in Scotland. Anyway, I have won my first Scottish cap—did you know?

"There is a big invitation race in South Africa in a month's time in which Lester Piggott has been invited to ride for England. Tony Murray for Ireland—and me for Scotland. So I am representing my country for the first time.

"A patriot? Yes, I'm proud of it!"

Willie Carson is the first to admit that Lester Piggott might still have been champion if he had not been riding so much on the international scene.

"Lester hasn't put up a big fight this year. He has not worked so hard as in the past. I've no doubt he could still have been champion if he had wanted. But he has gone after the money instead.

"I've been around Europe a bit myself this year—France, Italy, Germany, Norway and Sweden."

Now he attains the championship dream of every stable lad, earning more than he cares to say, but there is an even greater prize eluding him.

"I want to win the Derby for Lord Derby. Only great horses win that race and I've never had one of them—never been in with a shout."

What about all the talking that is said to go on between jockeys in a long-distance race? Is it friendly?

"I wouldn't exactly call it friendly," smiles Willie, "it's usually a case of somebody getting in the way and you're telling him to get out of it. It never comes to a fight but jockeys do have their arguments. There is still room for some fun in the weighing-room though."

There will be room for fun and reminiscence on Saturday when the Carson family get together.

Willie's father has now moved to a Fyffe's post at Norwich, within easy reach of the three grandchildren, Antony, Neil and Ross.

But Willie will be back in Scotland when he returns from South Africa in December, to see his grandfather, Rab Hunter, who has been ill in Stirling.

He may also manage to fit in a football match. For that was his favourite sport until racing took over. And Stirling Albion can chalk up Britain's No 1 jockey as their most distinguished fan.

GENTLE JOHNNY GOES FREE AT LAST

─────────────── *6th November 1972* ───────────────

Safe-blower Johnny Ramensky told a sheriff who deferred sentence on him that he didn't want to die in jail.

He got that wish. But it was only an ambulance journey to Perth Royal Infirmary which separated him from the prison surroundings which had become all too much a home to him.

He was still serving a sentence when he was taken on Friday to hospital, where he died, aged 67, on Saturday night.

So ended the life and remarkable criminal career of John Ramensky, who first fell foul of the law about the time of the Battle of the Somme. The temptation to blow a safe was still dogging him 56 years later.

In the intervening years, Gentle John, the Peter Pan of the "jelly" men, had amassed sentences of more than 50 years, escaped from the strict security of Peterhead Prison five times and enjoyed his greatest period of freedom during the war, when his genius was harnessed to the national emergency.

Ramensky the Commando was then parachuted behind enemy lines in Italy where he daringly blew open German safes and secured important papers.

It gave him a status in life—and earned him an honourable

discharge in 1945 with a special mention for "meritorious service".

But meritorious service of one day can be criminal activity the next, depending on how you direct your talents.

Ramensky, born of Lithuanian parents and later changing his name to Ramsay, was soon back in the old business, a connection with which he showed an almost touching reluctance to part.

Indeed his expert handling of explosives more or less condemned him to detection. Experienced detectives would walk into a safe-blowing scene and say without much hesitation: "Ay, ay, Johnny's been here."

As a relative said: "He was a craftsman who just refused to retire from his trade."

But Ramensky of the deep-set eyes and friendly, East-European face was failing.

His sight was not so good nor his footing so sure. Two years ago, he plunged 60 feet from a roof in Stirling while attempting a midnight break-in.

He spent 14 weeks in hospital, suffering from a fractured skull, thigh and wrist—and slightly dented pride—before facing the law.

John Ramensky is survived by his wife—they lived apart latterly—whose home is in the Gorbals.

THE FINAL OCTAVE

———————— *1st December 1972* ————————

The brightest Scottish light on the literary scene went out for ever in the dawn of yesterday, "quickly and quietly" as the bulletin said.

The news from Edinburgh seemed as unreal as it was saddening.

For death was the very antithesis of all that one associated with Sir Compton Mackenzie, prolific writer, keen thinker and talker and as sparkling and colourful a personality as Scotland has seen this century.

From that moment at eight months old, when he later claimed to have gained a remembered consciousness of life, until his death a few weeks short of his 90th birthday, the whole essence of the man was life, life, life.

It bubbled over from his inventive mind into his brilliant conversation; it shone from those dancing eyes even when they had lost their power to see.

To sit by the canopied, four-poster bed where he spent his forenoons—as I did not so long ago—was to be washed over by the refreshing waves of an inspired mind and golden tongue.

He detested pornography. He once said: "The sexy sixties

will go down as the most idiotic display in mankind's history. On sex we have lost our sense of proportion. To my mind the sex act, except for the two people involved, is fundamentally a comic opera."

He liked hand-made shirts and the good things of life. "All my life I've lived hand to mouth, damned good hand to mouth, mind you."

He never had enough money, which was one reason why, at the age of 80, he started on an ambitious 10-volume autobiography which came out in 10 *Octaves* covering the first 80 years of his life.

The man who was a literary figure even before the First World War with books like *Sinister Street* and had turned out well over 100 more, including the memorable *Whisky Galore*, was himself a living history book.

Much of it he could relate so vividly either because he was there or knew someone who had told him about it. He remembered, for example, sitting on the knee of a man who gave him a first-hand account of Waterloo!

Despite an extraordinary life which had seen him as writer, soldier, Intelligence chief, Rector of Glasgow University, Britain's first-ever disc jockey and so much more, he was never one to dwell in the past.

He defined good conversation as "the exchange of experience, knowledge and opinion, sprinkled with Attic salt and enriched by the appropriate anecdote, well told."

The best conversation in English, he reckoned, could be heard in Edinburgh and Dublin. The best talkers, he thought, were incurable monopolists, more apt to spoil the art of conversation than to adorn it.

Sir Compton never spoiled it. He and his great friend, Lord Boothby, were the two best after-dinner speakers I ever heard. It was at a dinner honouring Boothby that I heard his finest performance, one which doubled up his audience with laughter for half-an-hour before turning them to utter silence for the serious point which he wished to make.

In the First World War he fought with the infantry and the Royal Marines, was wounded at the Dardanelles and was put in charge of Intelligence in the Aegean about which he later wrote with such candour that his book was withdrawn and he was convicted and fined for a breach of the Official Secrets Act.

He laid much more stress on the importance of mental activity than physical, claiming the advantage of not having taken any violent exercise since he was an Oxford undergraduate.

"I venture to speculate that golf may be responsible for a higher mortality rate than cigarettes," he used to say, mischievously recalling that while he had his first cigar butt at the age of four, he did not become a regular pipe smoker until 13!

Latterly, he spent all his time in Drummond Place, Edinburgh, with his third wife Lilian. His first wife died in 1960, after which he married his secretary, Christina MacSween. After she died in 1963, he married her sister, the present Lady Mackenzie. He had no family.

Sir Compton once said that "every man must decide for himself how to approach old age."

He set a good example by approaching it with optimism and humour and dignity, as well as a sense of having lived life to the full. He packed in enough experience to cover a dozen normal lives.

MODERN MILLIE WOULD MAKE
THE OLD LAIRD SMILE

——————————— *1st December 1972* ———————————

Once upon a time there was a Laird of Killiecrankie who rather disgraced himself in the family by marrying the servant girl. A few generations later that improbable union produced a descendant who turned out to be a musical comedy star of international fame.

And I suspect that most of the starch would have been taken out of the Killiecrankie frowns by the disarming personality of the girl in question—Millicent Martin.

Our thoroughly modern Millie sipped a refreshing drink and laughed about her background as she relaxed between rehearsal and final recording of a Scottish Television "Sound Stage" programme. It is one of those more costly items which STV hope to sell around the commercial network.

She was all enthusiasm for my suggestion that she might do a television programme from the family seat at Killiecrankie. But our conversation was centred on more recent history.

Like that controversial TV programme of 10 years ago, "That Was The Week That Was", which produced such new names to the entertainment scene as David Frost, William Rushton, Lance Percival—and, of course, Millie Martin.

How does she look back on that way-out event which

210

had a shattering effect on lives and reputations far beyond the studio doors?

"It was exciting to be involved in something new," says the vivacious red head. "Some of it went wrong but a lot of it went right. That type of show is dead now—or rather we bashed the hell out of it—and you cannot renew that kind of thing till much later.

"But part of its success was that it was live and spontaneous. It saddens me that most of television today is pre-recorded, because people liked being involved in something that could—and did—go wrong.

"It took risks—and it is death to anything if you're not prepared to take risks. That is why I sang recently in my first-ever light opera, *The Beggar's Opera* at Chichester. We did 98 per cent business and it was a marvellous experience."

That was simply the latest departure in a varied career which has stretched far longer than most people realise. Though the turning point in her career came with TW3, Millicent Martin was, in fact, dancing as a chorus girl 22 years ago.

Without knowing it, I saw her in the dancing-line of *Blue for a Boy* (remember Fred Emney?) in London's West End in 1950.

"I danced in choruses for five years, which gave me a good grounding," she recalls. "That included a run in *South Pacific* at Drury Lane. Actually, the girls of *South Pacific* have a reunion every three or four years and we are having one on Friday first.

"From dancing they asked me to sing in a musical and I fell in love with singing from then on. If I had to choose a career in show business, I think I would have preferred to have been a second lead rather than a bigger name. That way you can work all the time. As it is, I have to think carefully about the engagements I accept.

211

"In fact, I don't take a part just for the money in it. I take what I enjoy doing and that means that I usually work for about six months in the year.

"Television has remained my first love and I have done some films, like *Alfie* and *Stop the World*.

"But every now and then you must go back to the stage to keep your sense of timing. Audiences give you that. So I did the opera and I am due in the Birmingham pantomine, *Puss in Boots*."

It all fits in which the career of her husband, actor Norman Ashley, whom she married three years ago after her marriage to singer Ronnie Carroll was dissolved. They have a house in London and a flat in Brighton.

The director called and Millie was off for that final recording. I could not help recalling the pert, bouncy girl of "That Was The Week That Was".

And contrasting her with the more mature, sophisticated woman of 38 who was now appearing on the monitor screen with a seductive, swivelling movement to match the mood of "Hey Big Spender".

GREAT GRANDAD'S WOOIN'
STILL WOWS 'EM

——————— *6th December 1972* ———————

It was Robert Louis Stevenson who once forecast that the dialects of Scotland would fade out in his own lifetime. Admittedly, he expired before his time but the judgment was still far from accurate.

For the spoken Scots lives on. And, if I had needed any proof of the fact, I would have found it in a village hall in Aberdeenshire the other evening when local people crowded in to enjoy that classic of northern rural drama, *Mains's Wooin'*.

It is a musical play in the unmistakable dialect of the North-East, rich and expressive and still spoken and received with meaning and understanding.

By coincidence, *Mains's Wooin'*, a comedy of country life and loves, was written in the very year of Stevenson's death—1894—and has enjoyed so many revivals that the breath has never been out of it.

It was written by a noted Aberdeenshire scholar, Gavin Greig, closely related to Edvard Grieg, the composer, whom Norway claims as her own, even though his family was rooted at Cairnbulg, near Fraserburgh, before crossing the sea, and changing the "Greig" to "Grieg".

213

Gavin Greig had a few less distinguished relatives like myself (I am his great-grandson), but he himself was an outstanding figure, writing operettas and plays which were much in vogue at the end of the century, as well as novels and poems.

Greig was the son of the forester from Parkhill of Dyce, near Aberdeen, graduating at Aberdeen University and settling, while still in his early twenties, as the schoolmaster at Whitehill, in the Buchan district of Aberdeenshire.

That first night of *Mains's Wooin'* was often described to me by the eldest of his 10 children, who was my grandmother. Soon the play spread itself around Scotland, and even into England, though how they made much sense of it I don't quite know.

But it went on and on and there we were, nearly 80 years later, enjoying it as if it were new. Just as the author had intended, the New Pitsligo Drama Group consisted of a rural cross-section from farmers like Bill Pratt and cattlemen like Jimmy Smith and Russell Lowe to a transport manager (Joe Ritchie) and a village grocer (Alfie Johnston).

I had been invited there, as a direct descendant, to address an audience I had grown up with, and I recalled to them that since the first performance in 1894, we had come through from the shelt and gig, the bicycle, motor-car and airplane to the rocket on the moon.

But I found it rather appealing that, basically, people themselves had changed very little. As an audience, we were reacting to recognisable humour and hypocrisies and romantic notions that seemed fresh and eternal.

I appealed to the audience to fight off the snobbish notion that dialect words are playground vulgarity—and to encourage their children to learn that rich and meaningful and worthwhile culture alongside their English.

The response to that plea was such an enthusiasm of

applause that I knew, there and then, that the Doric of Scotland was far from dead.

CRATER DOCTOR TELLS
OF MASSACRE ESCAPE

———————— 8th December 1972 ————————

The date was June 20, 1967, and trouble was boiling up in Aden, as an over-flow from the Arab-Israeli Six-Day War.

An advance party of the Argyll and Sutherland Highlanders was taking over from the Northumberland Fusiliers and a joint patrol had set out to investigate some incident in the volcanic enclosure city of Crater.

With that patrol was Dr Tom Kenyon, the Argyll's medical officer. Suddenly, at the entrance to Crater Dr Kenyon was called back to a sick man.

And that was how he escaped from the notorious Crater Massacre, in which the rest of the party drove on to a horrible death.

"As medical officer I had to take delivery of those men who had been tortured to death," says the doctor, who is now free to give this detailed account because he recently left the Army.

"I had gone back to Main Pass, Crater, to within a few hundred yards of these men, only to find that Army top-brass had withheld permission to use main armament in their rescue.

"Before that incident, I had had an innocent respect for

216

politicians. I never imagined that I could feel ashamed to wear a British uniform.

"But that was how I felt that day. These British soldiers had been sacrificed for political reasons—reasons which those of us on the ground knew to be totally false.

"The Arabs interpreted all this as meaning that the British were afraid."

And that bloody incident, the prelude to the recapture of Crater by Colonel Colin Mitchell and his Argylls, was a main factor in turning the thoughts of Dr Kenyon to another battle—the political one.

He was so incensed by the Labour Government's exposure of British troops in Aden, in the interests of not upsetting the Arabs, that he decided he would fight them one day.

And that, in a nutshell, is the story behind a headline the other day which told us that he was Tory candidate to contest Kelvingrove at the next General Election.

Dr Kenyon went on: "On that notorious June 20, I had already dealt with the bodies of eight other British soldiers in another shooting incident.

"Back in Crater, the men I left had been ambushed by terrorists and armed police, dragged through the streets before jeering crowds who played football with parts of their bodies.

"Eventually, 12 bodies, burned and tortured, came out on the back of a lorry. The remains of three were stuffed in a packing case. The Arabs tried to tell me it was goats' meat. It was, of course, our own soldiers."

Dr Kenyon, born in Lancashire, had gone from a post in Raigmore Hospital, Inverness, into the Army, establishing himself happily in the "family" setting of the Scottish infantry regiment.

When he later left the Argylls, he became a parachute-trained operator with the highly-skilled Special Air Service.

He then moved to Northern Ireland, working at the internment camp at Gerwood Park and on the prison ship *Maidstone*.

But if Dr Kenyon was incensed by Labour's policy in Aden, he is not exactly falling over himself in support of current Tory policy in Ulster.

He said: "I believe there is no political solution to Northern Ireland and that law and order must be enforced. Once that happens, the pond of the terrorist fish will dry up."

Dr Kenyon has left the Army and comes back to the land of the Argylls, where he has many friends, to take over a practice in the north of Glasgow in partnership with his wife. Their home is in Stirling.

Colin Mitchell, better known as "Mad Mitch", who crossed top brass over the conduct of the Aden campaign and was so blatantly snubbed that he quit the Army in disgust, now sits as Tory Member for West Aberdeenshire.

And his former medical officer has plans to join him in the political front-line.

CARRICK AHOY!

———————— *11th January 1973* ————————

The lunchtime bustle of a Glasgow club was at its height yesterday when I incurred the displeasure of George Watson.

George, a fine old salt with an appealing absence of teeth, is the doorman who asked me, in the way that doormen do: "Take your coat, sir?"

"It's all right," I replied, "I'll take it upstairs with me."

"Oh, you can't do that here, sir. Not here you can't," he said with tones of distaste. "Coats are left down below."

In my ignorance, I had, in fact, boobed twice. Old George winced visibly when I mentioned 'upstairs', as he explained to me later.

"Companionway, sir not 'staircase'. Always companionway in a ship."

Thus, improved in my nautical manners, I set about exploring the good ship *Carrick*.

She's the oldest British ship still afloat, one-time wool clipper and now the premises of the Royal Naval Volunteer Reserve Club of Scotland, berthed on the Clyde.

She was built in 1864 for the Australian wood trade under her original name of *City of Adelaide* and set up a record passage for clippers by doing the Adelaide-London run in

65 days.

Nearly 25 years ago, she came in to rest on the quiet waters of the Clyde to offer a familiar recreation point for the naval officers just back from the war.

Today, there are fewer of the breed and the 1,500 members include a fair proportion of land-lubbers who become associate members through friendship with those already there.

But, says club secretary Walter Strang: "Most of the members still have some connection with the sea—yachts and that kind of thing."

SO POETIC, YOU SCOTS, SAYS ROBERT GRAVES

———————— *25th January 1973* ————————

Robert Graves, one of the great poets of the century, and writer of some of the finest lyric verse in the English language, was back in Scotland yesterday for the first time since 1916.

That year they had left him for dead in the Battle of the Somme, his colonel writing to tell his mother of a glorious and heroic son. But Graves lived.

His visit to Scotland was as military escort to another great poet, Siegfried Sassoon, who had had a nervous breakdown.

"I was bringing him to see a head-shrinker in Edinburgh, and it was on that visit that I also met Wilfred Owen, the poet, who was also suffering from a break-down," he told me. "Owen was cured, only to be killed at the very end of the war.

"It was really time for me to see Scotland again. The reason I haven't been back is because nobody invited me," he laughed.

Well, somebody has invited him now—Scottish Television, for whom tonight he will propose "The Immortal Memory of Robert Burns", on the Bard's anniversary.

Large and flowing, with the bulk of a heavyweight boxer and the head of a Roman emperor, Robert Graves, at 77, has been a distinguished citizen of Majorca since 1929.

The guide books mention him as a kind of historic monument and coach drivers stop to point him out.

But Graves, former Professor of Poetry at Oxford, is very much a living monument to the power of words, half in a world of his own but always ready to test your knowledge with a sudden question. There is a sort of crusty kindliness about him.

How, I wondered, does a great poet of the twentieth century view the nation which produced Robert Burns? Is there still relevance in a Bard whose world of Cottar's Saturday Nights, from which Auld Scotia's grandeur sprang, is hardly with us any more?

"We no longer have the things of Shakespeare's day either but he is still relevant," says Robert Graves. "Yes, Burns is a great poet of Scotland, just as Shakespeare is of England. But, then, you are a poetic nation.

"Dunbar was the father of Scottish poetry and you have had such people as Lady Nairne, who was really fantastic.

"To me, however, the most extraordinary thing about the Scots is that they have a strange power to give life to inanimate objects. Kipling was wise enough to spot this and to emphasise it.

"If you have a breakdown with your car, for example, the Scot will somehow manage to get it to the garage."

But isn't that no more than an aptitude for engineering, I ventured.

"It has an engineering application but, believe me, it is far more a poetic power than an engineering power," said Graves earnestly. "It is a kind of driving force, a form of magic which no other nation in the world possesses. I cannot explain it; it is quite strange but it is true."

Robert Graves went to live in Majorca to pursue his own "secret vice" of poetry, having written his famous autobiographical *Goodbye To All That*, which gave the world a new catch-phrase.

"I went on the recommendation of two people—Lawrence of Arabia, the most extraordinary man I have ever known, and Gertrude Stein, who said to me: 'Majorca is Paradise, if you can take it.'

"Well, it is no longer Paradise but it is still my home. There used to be 2,000 visitors a year; now there are six million. The house I built for £2,000 would now fetch £50,000.

Sometimes his thoughts turn back to Britain which gave him birth.

"Of course there are far too many cars and too few bicycles," he says, "but things here are pretty good when you consider what other countries are like. In Britain, money doesn't completely run the country, as happens elsewhere.

"The younger generation are pretty damn-good, in my view, again when you compare them with the same generation elsewhere.

"I used to go to America quite a lot but not any more. All this business of mugging and people wanting to give you a fix."

Robert Graves, the poet who came out of exile to talk of Robert Burns, stuck a flat hat on his head—and went out to take his first look at Scotland in 57 years.

JENNY, AT 70, OFF TO A
BED-SITTER IN ESKIMO-LAND

———————— *6th February 1973* ————————

Jenny Gilbertson is 70, small and wiry, with complexion and teeth all her own and eyes that dance and sparkle like a Highland stream.

With her knitting needles and air of homeliness, she could readily constitute the portrait of a Scottish grandmother.

Except that the picture gets a little out of focus when you consider that, in 1970, she left her Shetland home, her daughters and grandchildren and went off to live with the Eskimos in the North West Territory of Canada.

She went for two or three months and stayed for nearly three years. And now that she is back in her more familiar surroundings, it is only to see her family and attend to a few business details before heading off back into the wild and frozen north of North America, where the warmest of welcomes awaits her on Southampton Island.

For Jenny Gilbertson, a widow, has been completely accepted into the Eskimo fold, having proved herself by venturing out across the frozen waters on seal and walrus hunts, exposed to the full hazards of Eskimo life.

"I never really thought of it as courageous," said the bright little lady as she sat by a Shetland fireside, "but I suppose it was a bit hazardous, when you come to think of it. It was so cold, for a start.

"Then, when we were out hunting and ice was starting to break up, we had to get the dogs across the open cracks. Sometimes we just had to throw them into the water and they had to swim for it."

The missing link in the story so far is the fact that Jenny Gilbertson is a first-class photographer, indeed one of the unsung and underpaid pioneers of woman-behind-the-camera.

Her film, *The Rugged Island*, which was in demand around the British cinemas in 1935, meant more than professional success. In making it, she enlisted the aid of a Shetland blacksmith-crofter who became guide, assistant and friend.

John Gilbertson also became husband and that, in a sense, diverted her from the other passion of her life.

"I used to go round lecturing, while John worked the projector, but he didn't really like the life. Then the children came and the filming was stopped," says Jenny.

But the interest in filming never left her. After her husband died she struck up a friendship with another distinguished resident of Shetland, Elizabeth Balneaves, the writer and artist, and the two ladies planned a joint expedition to the land of the Eskimos.

Once in Canada, Miss Balneaves took pneumonia and had to abandon her part in the adventure. So the widow from Shetland went ahead alone.

The Canadian Broadcasting Corporation have snapped up her *Eskimo Children*, her *Arctic Dog Teams* and a film about the hunting community, as well as her *Shetland Ponies*, and she is currently in touch with the BBC about showing her work in this country.

Then it's off back to her "bed-sitter" in Eskimo land—

no, not to an igloo any more but to one of the sectional houses provided by the Canadian Government.

RODDY REKINDLES THAT VITAL SPARK

—————————— *6th March 1973* —————— —

As with most things familiar in this life, the palate for television becomes jaded after a time. It takes more and more to amuse and entertain us, less and less to make cynics of us.

So, when something finally succeeds in stimulating the taste-buds, the vibrations are doubly pleasurable.

And that was my experience last night when "The Vital Spark" (BBC1) turned out to be the vital spark indeed. It was Para Handy and his crew, of course, resurrected for a once-only airing as part of BBC Scotland's 50th anniversary week.

And one is immediately prompted to wonder why it takes any kind of excuse to produce a gem like this.

One is then stirred to something nearer impatience to discover that the gentle delights of these Clydeside salts and their ramshackle puffer, plying between Greenock and Arran, are not considered of sufficient interest to English viewers.

Instead, the southern British were being treated to yet another saga of marriage break-up.

They seem less partial to things Scottish. Yet I swear last night's programme would have been understood and thoroughly enjoyed as far apart as Margate and Manhattan.

That excellent script of Bill Craig was skilfully directed by Pharic McLaren and brilliantly acted by some of those fine talents which currently grace the Scottish theatre.

We found them all invited to a wedding—all, that is, except Macphail the engineer (John Grieve), whose offence over the omission sent him scurrying to the "booze boutique" for the Dutch courage by which he could scuttle his mates' chances of getting to the church on time.

His subsequent work-to-rule meant minimum stoking and minimum speed overcome in time by Sunny Jim, the deck-hand (Alex McAvoy) throwing lumps of coal down the funnel!

Para Handy (Roddy McMillan), busily preparing his pompous speech for the wedding was knocked speechless when Macphail had the effrontery to describe *The Vital Spark* as "an old chanty."

He saw it as a noble ship and his position as a noble calling, comparable to that of Mister McGubbin, the minister (Fulton Mackay).

As he told the puzzled cleric on the voyage to the wedding: "You are calling up there for mercy and I'm calling down here for more steam."

The final arrival on Brodick Pier was marked with a runaway bogey scene, worthy of the Keystone Cops, which ended with Macphail and the parson in the casualty ward of the cottage hospital — where the wedding ceremony was finally performed.

So all's well that ends unwell.

Now, what about a series of shorter episodes going out to the whole network?

LINKLATER: THE START OF
A SLIGHTLY DIFFERENT CHAPTER

—————————— *2nd April 1973* ——————————

Eric Linklater, Scottish novelist whose wit and wisdom have delighted the reading public for half a century, drew a sweeping hand across the view from his front window and invited me to share his enthusiasm for the absence of people.

His horror of an over-crowded world, which will be doubling its numbers inside another life-time, was heightened on a return visit to Bombay, where he was once an assistant editor on *The Times of India*.

"I had known Bombay as an attractive city but now it is bursting at the seams, with people sleeping on the pavements. Calcutta is worse.

"So we are uncommonly fortunate in this part of the world to be free of that kind of problem. We are also fortunate to be far more reasonable people than you will find in many parts of the earth.

"We don't do anything to excess. Even crime in Glasgow is pretty much exaggerated. I have a son who has gone there to train and he likes it so much that he intends to stay on and teach in the city."

Eric Linklater sold off his beautiful mansion in Easter Ross to the oil-builders, who were invading his peace, and has

229

found another haven on the estate of Haddo House, the home of Lord Aberdeen.

That brings him back to familiar territory. It was from Aberdeen Grammar School, which also produced Lord Byron, that the young Linklater made off to do battle in the glaur of the First World War.

A bullet went through his helmet, traversed the interior of his Nordic skull and emerged through the other side of his helmet, leaving him with a permanent wound—and a title for a later autobiography *Fanfare For a Tin Hat*. He keeps the old hat as a memento.

It was the start of a fascinating adult life-span which took him to America during the years of Prohibition and produced such popular novels as *Juan in America*, *Private Angelo* and *Poet's Pub*.

"But I doubt if there will be any more novels. I have managed to keep myself by writing for more than 45 years and, fortunately, nobody goes on forever. Though I was never in the rip-roaring best-seller class, I did jolly well for a long time.

"But the faculty of invention fades out of existence and I also find that I have grown lazy in my old age." (He is 74.) "In any case, the sort of novels people read nowadays are not the sort I would want to write.

"Instead, I have been persuaded by my old friend, Bernard Fergusson, to write a history of the Black Watch.

"There is a lot of careless writing around today. I have always made it my habit to read aloud to myself what I have written because I believe that writing should have a natural rhythm and that, if you cannot speak it easily and naturally, there is something wrong with it."

On the current revolution of oil and its effect on his beloved Scotland, Eric Linklater has mixed feelings.

"There is no Highland authority which would turn down

the kind of employment opportunities which are being offered. And the wages are tremendously good.

"But I wish the Government could do something to slow down the pace of oil development, because a good deal of all this is bound to be experimental.

"No one has had the experience of drilling in seas as rough as they will find off Shetland, and I believe that the dangers of serious accident could be greatly reduced.

"There is also no doubt that a lot of most attractive landscape in Scotland is going to be ruined beyond any possibility of repair with some of these excavations. You won't be able to get rid of the evidence of 30 years of intensive industry.

"Aberdeen has been a market town on the grand scale but it cannot retain that character with a huge influx of industry."

Eric Linklater spends much of his time re-reading books— "It's like looking up old friends"—and he will tell you of a certain appreciation of the fact that his lifetime has co-incided with such a varied period of history.

Of that First World War which he has described to the detail of screaming, wounded horses, he says: "It was intensely dramatic to see field guns going into action while pulled by the horse. Do you know that the weight of fodder brought into France to feed them actually exceeded the weight of ammunition?"

The noise and stench of it all are but distant echoes in the mind of a man who has more often turned away to the comic situations of life for relief.

That war gave him an early lesson about life and living which deepened his compassion. To our gain, it did nothing to blunt his wit.

INTO ORBIT WITH
MOON MAN PATRICK

6th April 1973

As the leg-spin bowler of Selsey cricket team, he would scarcely rate a mention in his local paper.

As the man who has turned astronomy into an understandable and fascinating subject for the masses, there are few to compare with Patrick Moore, that great lumbering lump of a chap whose writings and television programmes continue to delight the millions.

With characteristic enthusiasm he came breezing into Glasgow this week to open an exhibition of Arthur Frank's magnificent collection of early scientific instruments—and packed the Art Gallery for the occasion.

Hordes of youngsters swarmed round for autographs, a clear indication of the tremendous impact of this wartime navigator of airplanes who has since become a navigator of public attention in the regions of the Great Unknown.

When I finally tracked him down in the orbits of adulation, it was not hard to know his appeal. For Patrick Moore, a bachelor of 50, combines the ruggedness of adventure with a gentle and courteous manner which finds time and a word for everyone.

As a larger-than-life eccentric he laughs heartily at the

suggestion, once made, that Patrick Moore gives the impression of having been hastily constructed. He will add to the mirth with examples of his physical clumsiness.

But there is nothing clumsy about the mind. From the age of six, when his mother gave him a book on the subject, he has been hooked on astronomy.

Heart trouble in childhood meant that most of his schooling took place at home, so he read and observed and became an authority without the intrusion of university degrees.

To this day he regards himself as a borderline case, a professional writer about an amateur study.

Once we had made a soft landing on an easy-chair away from the crowds, I invited Mr Moore to expound on his favourite subject. What about the moon now. What's in prospect when the Americans are about to launch Skylab, the plan to put a laboratory into space—and upon which so much of the future of space exploration depends?

"The moon, of course, has always been my main interest because, when I was young, it was an entirely amateur province," he began. "I was a pre-war moon mapper, and some of these were used in the early space research programmes. In the future I believe there will still be large-scale scientific travel to the moon, with lunar bases, but I don't see holidays on it or anything like that.

"A lot depends now on Skylab. If that goes well and there are no tragedies, then we may well see men on Mars by the end of the century. I wouldn't rule it out.

"But there is no life there except perhaps a low type of organic life. Nor is there life anywhere else in our own particular solar system. I believe, however, that there must be life in other systems, perhaps on millions of planets— and of a higher order than we know on earth.

"Actual travel to these places will be out of the question, but we will probably get to know about it all in time, though it will have to be by methods of which we know nothing at present."

What does Patrick Moore say to people who condemn space programmes on the basis that there are enough problems on earth without bothering about elsewhere?

"I tell them to go and do their homework, because they must be pretty ignorant to say a thing like that. Once they start investigating they learn—though some people never learn—that there are medical advantages for a start.

"Then there is the saving of life from the weather satellites, which give advance warning of these tropical storms. And perhaps most important of all, there will be tremendous international co-operation as a result of things like the moon bases, which will be jointly run.

"These people will be learning to co-operate, irrespective of what the politicians are doing."

Mr Moore rearranges his considerable girth and recalls how the BBC, looking for someone to present a programme on astronomy, invited him for a trial of three. That was in April, 1957—and "The Sky at Night" has been running non-stop ever since!

His next exciting project will be to journey to Africa for the total eclipse of the sun due on June 30.

Countless converts have found that Patrick Moore is ever ready with personal encouragement. There was the schoolboy enthusiast who called at his home one day, asking if he could see his space equipment. The same boy recently became a professor of astronomy at an overseas university.

In Glasgow this week, he was supplying preliminary details—and a gust of enthusiasm—for a planetarium, which is very much in the mind of the civic amenities convener Mrs Constance Methven.

SIR WILLIAM—OUT OF
THE LION'S MOUTH

—————————— *13th April 1973* ——————————

The tall, athletic figure of Sir William Collins swept into Glasgow yesterday, after his latest trip around the world in search of good books.

The man who once survived an encounter with Elsa the lioness, in which his head was in the animal's mouth, was back on safer ground.

Back, in fact, to Cathedral Street, where he started work in the family publishing business more than 50 years ago.

As head of that firm, he will step across the street to Strathclyde University today, when he will receive an honorary doctorate and open the new Collins building in memory of his cousin.

It will be a proud moment for a great Scot. The same man who sent the name of Collins round the world was a Wimbledon tennis player, an outstanding cricketer—and was all set to play his first game as a Queen's Park footballer when he damaged his ankle while running for a Glasgow tramcar.

Perhaps a man born in the tumultuous week of Mafeking's relief was destined for an eventful life. Though nearing his 73rd birthday, he still plays tennis and golf and goes surfing—but is still a youngster compared to his mother who lives happily in Troon, aged 93.

An interesting job, however, is the mainspring which keeps Sir William Collins as fresh and active and youthful as most men half his age.

In 1934, with the mission of building up a list of new books and authors, he moved from Glasgow to the London office to join his uncle, Sir Godfrey Collins, Liberal M.P. for Greenock, who became Secretary of State for Scotland in the Ramsay MacDonald Government of the Thirties.

Today, Sir William lives in a flat above the offices in St James's Place.

"But a publisher nowadays cannot sit around as a figure-head," he says. "You must find books and, having done that, you must mix your interest between editorial, promotion and sales.

"Personally, I get out and about, to the bush of Africa or wherever. I'm just back from a tour which took in Australia and New Zealand and included a visit to a young Scotsman, Robert Bustard from Alyth in Perthshire, who is turtle farming in the north of Australia.

"The turtle seems to have a strong appeal to people but it is becoming quite rare. Now Bustard is writing a couple of books about it.

"Then I went to India to see K. H. Sandkhala about the tiger. Do you know that in India, where it comes from, the tiger population has dropped from perhaps 30,000 about 15 years ago to around 2,000 now?

"Now, Mr Sankhala has been appointed head of Project Tiger, to save it, and he is writing a definitive book of the animal. Mrs Gandhi is doing the introduction."

Sir William published *Born Free* and the other Joy Adamson titles. But what about that encounter with Elsa?

"She got into my tent during the night, broke my mosquito

net and was apparently trying to get me out so that she could get her cubs in. At one stage I was on my back with my head in her mouth.

"It was very frightening but fortunately George Adamson managed to get her out."

Sir William recalls with some amusement the day he saw a short story he liked and which prompted him to say to the author: "Now you must write a novel."

"Never," said the man. But he must have had second thoughts. Some time later a manuscript landed on Sir William's desk. It was "H.M.S. Ulysses," by Alistair MacLean! Collins sold 250,000 copies in three months.

Collins books are produced in Glasgow by a staff of 3,000 who are gradually being moved out from the city centre to new premises at Bishopbriggs.

There's a touch of family dignity about it all, an insistence that individuals matter. Sir William's elder son is vice-chairman, his younger son looks after the paperback off-shoot, Fontana, and Lady Collins masterminded the recent achievement of producing a Common Bible, which has drawn Christians of all denominations that much closer.

The novel, says Sir William, will survive but the public are searching for good, readable stories and are not so interested in "problem" subjects of the day, as people seem to imagine.

They want relaxation and if a budding author can turn out something along the lines of a Howard Spring he'll do himself a service. Sir William's finger is firmly enough on the pulse of public taste to know.

And he has just produced a record profit of more than £3 million to prove it.

FAREWELL TO THE CHIEFTAIN

———————14th April 1973———————

A volley of rifle shots from the men of his old regiment sent the remains of the 11th Duke of Argyll, chief of Clan Campbell, on their last journey across Loch Awe to the beautiful islet of Inishail yesterday.

And there they were buried by the Cistercian Nunnery, close to the ruins of the very first castle the Campbells ever owned.

Kilted aristocrats and douce estate folk, veiled women and men on sticks clustered round the edge of the loch as the procession of six rowing boats moved out across the deep, dark waters from the private jetty at Ardanaiseig on a funeral cortege as simple and impressive as Scotland has ever seen.

In the first little boat, white and gleaming in the spring light, his widow, Mathilda, the dowager duchess, sat straight and serene, with the casket, one oarsman and the late Duke's personal piper, Ronald McCallum, balancing himself at the helm and playing the lament *My Home*.

They were followed by the new Duke and Duchess of Argyll, Lord Colin Campbell, the other son, Lady Jean Campbell, his daughter, and several relatives.

Estate workers rowed them into the distance complete

with wreaths of flowers and the Campbell standard of black and gold.

The atmosphere had been one of family occasion from the moment the mourners arrived from Inveraray Castle at the mansion house of Ardanaiseig.

There they were led through trees and down a terraced pathway to the water's edge by Piper Robert Stewart, formerly of the Argylls, as he played *The Flowers of the Forest*.

Behind him were the heraldic figures of the Ormonde Pursuivant and Sir Iain Moncrieffe of that Ilk, and the dowager duchess and members of the family.

Sir George Malcolm of Poltalloch represented Lord Maclean, the Lord Chamberlain and Lord Lieutenant of Argyll.

Behind again came the soldiers of the First Battalion the Argyll and Sutherland Highlanders, lining up at the pier, resplendent in kilt and green tunic and firing off their gun salute with the splendid precision which one expects from the men of the Thin Red Line.

For Ian Douglas Campbell it was all but over. Although he used to attend the Presbyterian Church at Inveraray, there was no religious ceremony.

Instead, little Donald Mackechnie, the session clerk at Inveraray, called out: "There will now be one minute's silence for personal prayer."

The 11th Duke was sailing off from a world which had brought him his share of joys and heartaches. Behind him now were such bleak years as those spent in a German prisoner of war camp after the collapse at St Valery.

Behind him, too, the turbulence of personal affairs, including much publicised divorce actions.

Indeed, controversy had followed him to the very hour of death, with a Parliamentary question about his return from the tax havens of France to a Scottish hospital.

The Hereditary Master of the Royal Household in Scotland, Keeper of the Great Seal of Scotland—the Admiral of the Western Coast and Isles—was sailing away from it all.

On Friday the 13th he was taking a last, leisurely voyage on waters which were troubled no more. All that was left was the peace and quiet of the Argyll hills and hollows.

It was really as good a day as any to come home for good.

BOUNCING BANKS HEADING
FOR HIS SECOND MILLION

—————————— *2nd May 1973* ——————————

The door to his private room says "Mr John Banks". Inside, Britain's most colourful millionaire is still the same fast-talking, Runyonish character whose razor-sharp shrewdness and bubbling enthusiasm took him from Glasgow tenement kid to Britain's most flamboyant bookmaker by the time he was 30.

Today, at 38, the material trappings are much the same, give or take a new sauna or the latest stereophonic wonder. There is still the millionaire mansion in Berkshire's Sunningdale, just along the road from the Duke of Windsor's old home at Fort Belvidere.

The Rolls still cocks a snook at the Mercedes in the driveway by the swimming pool and John Banks offers no apology for having spent the punter's money a good deal more wisely than the punter himself.

The big difference in his life, of course, is the fact that he is bookmaker no longer, having changed horses in midstream, so to speak, and come over on the side of the punter.

With the sale of his chain of betting shops to Maxwell Joseph's City Tote Group in a million-pound deal, he opened up the John Banks International Sporting Club last

September.

And next week, the ebullient Banks, who used to play the drums in Glasgow's Locarno Ballroom, comes bounding back from London to his native city to open up a Scottish branch of his new organisation.

It will look out across the Clyde from the Anderston district which reared him.

It's a dramatic change for the man who first caught the public eye in the sixties by accepting bets on Perry Mason losing a case, on who killed *The Fugitive*, on whether it would rain next Wednesday.

When Ross County met Rangers in the Scottish Cup, he offered to take kippers instead of money—and his office stank for weeks!

Doesn't he miss the glamour of the betting rails?

"Not at all," says Banks, with the same kind of fatalistic gesture he would use when paying his £80,000 of personal income tax. I'm still deeply involved in the one business I love—horse-racing and gambling—and I'm much more relaxed.

"Whereas I was once just a millionaire, I'm now a happy millionaire. I go to the race-course when I want to go, without the pressure of having to get up on that stool. Why, I even have time to take afternoon tea now.

"And I am free of the worry of clients and their bad debts. Bookmakers don't have the backing of the law in this matter. In my new venture you are not bothered with credit. People pay in advance.

"And I can tell you it's the best business I have ever tried. I've already ploughed back money, but in the first full year I reckon I'll show a bigger profit than ever I did as a bookmaker.

"Gambling in this country, you see, is much bigger than people, even those in authority, realise.

And Banks will not be losing on account of having closed his book. So what is the new business which brings him so much happiness as well as money?

Already there are 7,000 members (including a large number of doctors and an eye-opening proportion of priests!) paying a basic £10 to join.

It entitled them, for example, to take part in a fabulous outing to Longchamp for the Grand Prix de l'Arc de Triomphe (cost £15) or the trip to Las Vegas for the Bugner-Muhammad Ali fight. A party from Edinburgh took advantage of that offer, living in the same hotel where Ali was sparring—and all for around £200.

The John Banks nose for business is seldom wrong. Hard on the heels of his Glasgow office comes a Liverpool branch and soon after that he will be opening up in Jamaica, where there is a tremendous interest in British horse-racing.

He has cut down on his race-horse ownership and has branched into breeding, with 17 brood mares and nine foals.

But there is still a racehorse for his glamorous wife, Anne Marie.

"I think there's a fair chance that you'll see her as a jockey in the new ladies' racing," he smiles. "She may not be the best jockey but she'll damn well be the best-looking one!"

And he sparkles with the kind of bounce and enthusiasm which, he knows in the heart of Banks, will take him on to his second million.

SET FOR A NEW SOCCER ERA . . .
THAT'S STEIN!

————————— 5th May 1973 —————————

He rose from the grime and sweat of the Lanarkshire coalmines to become a phenomenon of football, moulding with the skill of a great artist the first British team to win the premier prize of European football.

Today, Jock Stein of Celtic is, arguably, the best Soccer manager in the world. He might also go down as the most significant figure in the entire history of Scottish football.

His record of eight league championships and a string of cup successes in his eight years with Celtic amount to one thing. His influence upon the standards of play, the conduct of players and the general thinking about the game are yet another.

So what more can one say? In this week of the Scottish Cup Final, when he is poised for possible additions to the laurels, I went along to Celtic Park to update myself on the power of Stein.

At 50, he is still the same large and likeable hunk of a man, hoarse voiced, warm of manner or ruthless according to requirement, with a passion for the idea that football and life are all about people.

He is quick to praise and equally quick to tear off strips,

even in public, when something bugs him. The acquired sophistications of worldly experience cannot win all the time!

But little of the man might ever have been known had it not been for a curious turn of fate in 1951.

Until then, Jock Stein, coal miner from Burnbank, near Hamilton, lived quietly on the borders of obscurity. The weekday grind of the pits was relieved by the exercise of playing for the lowly Albion Rovers on a Saturday, a pattern which continued from 1942 to 1950.

In that year, Big Jock went off to the greater wilderness of Llanelly, a non-League club in Wales, which seemed like the dying days of an undistinguished playing career.

Meanwhile, Glasgow Celtic had run into a series of bad injuries and desperately needed a stop-gap centre half. But who?

Up spoke old Jimmy Gribben, a faithful servant of the club, to say: "Whit aboot yon Stein wha used tae be wi' Albion Rovers?"

Whit aboot him, indeed? Except that somebody remembered him vaguely. He might do.

It only took a phone call and the modest Stein was heading back from the valleys of Wales for what was to be a belated run of glory as a player.

An ankle injury ended his playing days, but Stein, the moulder of men was born. He took over as coach to the Celtic reserves, branched out as manager of Dunfermline and Hibernian and followed his inevitable destiny to the manager's chair at Celtic Park in 1965.

In your wildest dreams, John Stein, you could never have imagined the unparalleled record of eight years later?

"No, it's not the sort of thing you believe will happen. But there was a nucleus of good players like McNeill, Murdoch, Johnstone, Lennox and Brogan, when I arrived in 1965 and all they needed was the taste of success.

"I brought in a few hungry players as well and I was lucky with my signings, like Joe McBride, Willie Wallace and Tommy Callaghan.

"Perhaps it is not so much the fact that I get the best out of people as the fact that they get the best out of me. Maybe we just complement each other. They always know that they will get a fair return.

"But football is about people, not just your players and officials and those closest to you. It's about those people who took the time and money to follow us to Edinburgh last Saturday for that vital game.

"They were just as enthusiastic as they were when we won our first championship in a final game with Motherwell.

"For as long as I see that my players are enthusiastic about success, then it doesn't lose its flavour for me. Mind you, we have no automatic right to it just because we happen to be a Celtic or a Rangers or a Liverpool."

Is there not a chance, I ventured, that the championship monopoly of one team might possibly knock the heart out of other teams and supporters and damage the game? Wouldn't a change do good?

"A change would do good only if Celtic were beaten by a better team," says Stein. "If that happened we would be the first to acknowledge it. If it wasn't a better team it wouldn't do the game any good at all.

"One of the troubles with Scottish football is that there are too many meaningless games in the First Division. Competition should be more geared to suit the population of the country and the needs of the people."

Stein likes to play down the strains of his position by telling you: "Ach, they work harder down the pits than we do here."

But the pressures are undeniable. Over the New Year, he was in the coronary care unit of Glasgow's Victoria Infirmary with the heart-strain of exhaustion.

It was time for public speculation about the future of the Big Man. Would he ease up? Perhaps do a "Matt Busby" and step upstairs to a less strenuous position?

"People might have ideas about the time for me to do something like that—last year or this year or whatever," he says. "But I'll be the one who will know best when the time comes. And that time is not imminent—no, not in the next two or three years.

"The trouble was that I didn't have a real holiday last year. I thought I could do with a holiday at home for a change—and I was wrong."

But Jock Stein is back, once more in full command of his team and fighting fit for the days ahead.

In his team for Saturday there are still some of those men who helped Celtic to their finest hour, in the European Cup Final of 1967.

Jock Stein, who seems poised for Phase Two of the great era, looks thoughtfully into an electric fire and says:

"Yes, we still have the remnants of the 1967 team—and remnants are worth having around you."

He didn't mean to be sentimental, I'm sure. But there was something sentimental in the way he said it.

WHY MEN FACE BLACK HELL

———————————— *12th May 1973* ————————————

In the sorrow that engulfs a nation when a pit disaster scars the headlines, one marvels again at the quality of courage which sends these men to the deep black bowels of the earth to earn a living.

What breed of man commits himself to a life divorced from God's light and dust-free air to howk his way through rugged rock for the sake of his bread and butter and pint of ale?

Ask a miner himself and he is liable to look at you blankly.

Just as the fisherman's son will take up the net and the farmer's son the plough, so is there a kind of reflex compulsion for the miner's son to lift the lamp.

Jock Stein of Celtic came out of the pits for the greater comforts of football. He says: "You go down because you are born in a mining area and there's nothing else for you. It's the tradition. My father was a miner and I followed him when I was 15. I stayed for 13 years, but it was a tough life. Yes, I was glad to see the back of it."

Jock Stein was one of many to emerge from the grimy depths, their muscles and character strengthened in a way that made them doubly fit for another challenge.

248

In football management alone, the list of ex-miners includes such names as Bill Shankly of Liverpool, and his brother Bob of Stirling, Jock Wallace of Rangers and Matt Busby of Manchester United.

In the ministry, there are men like the Rev Robert Cullen, of South Cathcart, Glasgow, and Father Clinton, curate of Govan St Francis. On the stage, there's Andrew Keir and in journalism, my own colleague, sports writer Jim Rodger.

Says Jim Rodger of his own days in the pits: "We worked against hazards of water and reek and foul air, without toilet facilities and in an atmosphere which would likely bring you silicosis, howking towards some seam of coal which would bring warmth to people's homes.

"When I left the pits, I found that I needed no taskmaster in life. My taskmaster is the Davy lamp which still sits on my desk."

The men who dig our coal can hardly be attracted by the money, which is short of spectacular. Nor by the comfort, though that has improved over the years.

Perhaps Jim Rodger strikes the point of the quiet, consolation which keeps men down the pits of Britain when present-day life offers alternatives which seem so preferable.

Of course, the weight of danger on men's heads is a well-known binding quality, the appeal of which explains the bouts of nostalgia in people who have lived through war.

Perhaps that's the kind of secret which buries itself in the marrow of the coal miner's soul. A secret which the five men of Fife now take with them to the tombs of Seafield Colliery, Kirkcaldy.

LOOKING BACK WITH
THE DAM BUSTER

———————— *16th May 1973* ————————

Wing Commander Guy Gibson and the crews of 19 Lancasters went roaring into the night sky from an English airfield. The date: May 16, 1943. The famous Dam Busters were on their way to raid the German Ruhr.

By next morning, they had blasted the vital Mohne, Eder and Sorpe Dams with the new-found bouncing bomb and flooded large areas of Germany's industrial war effort.

Gibson received the Victoria Cross and the Dam Buster raids became a legend of wartime heroism which has kept people talking every since.

There are those who marvel at the ingenuity of it all and, inevitably, there are those who make the assessments of a generation later and decide that it made little contribution to the ultimate defeat of the Germans.

But people are fascinated, not least the children of the '70s, whose wide-eyed wonder at *The Dam Busters* film encourages the TV companies to show it over and over again.

Few parents these days have escaped the questions about the pilots and the bombs and, most of all, about the man who thought it all up—Barnes Wallis.

A working apprentice by 1904, when the Wright Brothers

were taking to the air . . . inventor of the world's most beautiful airship, the R80, and the most successful, R100 . . . the man who gave us the Wellington and Wellesley bombers, the Tallboy and Grand Slam bombs, as well as the bouncing bomb, before extending himself to the supersonic age with the swing-wing plane and so much more.

Could such a man be still alive, as the records suggested?

In search of that proof, I drove up a sleepy lane in Surrey the other day to White Hill House—to spend an hour with Barnes Wallis in his den, full of pictures of the Mohne Dam, the R80 and R100, models, books and papers.

What about the attempts to minimise the importance of those Dam Buster raids?

"Well, of course, they were an absolute disaster for the Germans," he said, with a sense of affront that anyone should have doubted it.

"We killed between 1,000 and 2,000 people, swept away animals and crops and flooded their factories."

He assured me that he had no conscience about the killings on the other side. He knew that in the long term many more lives had been saved.

He was rummaging about the room, looking for this and that, knocking down a paint tin and finally coming up with the model of his famous 10-ton bomb.

That was the one which blasted the launching sites of V1 and V2 rockets and the German submarine pens along the French coast.

It also destroyed, with one strike from his Dam Buster boys, the vital Bielefeld Viaduct after 3,000 tons of American bombs had failed to scratch it.

The secret of the bomb, as he took pains to illustrate to me with inventor's excitement, was the slight angle of the tail-fins which put greater spin as it drilled its way into the target.

Sir Barnes—he had to wait until he was 80 before the nation put right the scandalous omission of his knight-hood—exploded the popular impression that there is bitterness in his soul because his genius was so often thwarted by stodgy bureaucracy.

"Not bitter at all," he assured me. "You see, there is a natural tendency in people to resist any kind of innovation. They don't like being pushed out of their conventional channel of life.

"The inventor is in a worse position because people cannot really gauge the effect of what he is on about. Besides, it is likely to be expensive.

"So there is opposition—but that is a good thing. It makes you go on to perfect your original idea and, if it is really worthwhile, the chap who opposes you has to give in at the end of the day."

Sir Barnes was feeling a little lost without Lady Wallis, who was away from home for a few days. He admitted so himself, as he showed me photographs of his wife and his parents and talked of them all with shining admiration.

There was a final irony to the wartime story of this living legend. In all the bombing of the London area, there was only one landed on Epsom. But the victims on that label were the father, sister and brother-in-law of Lady Wallis.

JOURNEY INTO SPACE . . . AND
THE DAY I SAW TWO SUNSETS

─────────────── *18th May 1973* ───────────────

The white dazzle of the sun blinded me at 1am yesterday
. . . and I swear not a drop of the hard stuff had passed my
lips!

The experience, however, was no less intoxicating. For
there I was, streaking across the Arctic Circle in Concorde
002 at twice the speed of sound, 11 miles high and at what
is normally regarded as the dead of night.

Behind was Prestwick Airport, the strict security check
and the walk across the tarmac to this majestic bird of man's
creation, long and white and aloof, the world's most expensive and controversial airliner.

The smell of kerosene has filled the nostrils and tension
pulled at the nerve-ends, as four Olympus giants thrust us
into a sensational take-off with what I am told was the engine
power of 10,000 Minis!

Concorde struck east to St Abb's Head then leftwards up
the East Coast of Scotland to hit a course between Norway
and Iceland which would take us right inside the Arctic
Circle.

In a matter of minutes, she had reduced the significance
of Mother Earth, and risen, hunched, into the blue-black

acres of infinity.

At the control are two Scots, John Cochrane and Eddie McNamara, whose work as test pilots took them south many years ago but whose parents still live in Ayr and Ardrossan respectively.

On board are two scientists from the National Physical Laboratory whose mass of equipment is assessing the gasses of the upper atmosphere.

The pilots want to take them as far north as possible, so we are about to penetrate to a point inside the Arctic region from which we can view the sun over the top of the world as it warms our cousins in Australia.

I crouch on the flight deck, just behind the two pilots, as Concorde leaves the shade of a Scottish night and takes us towards a horizon of sunrise colours, a spectrum which runs from shades of blue to the gold and reds of a forest fire. Bing Crosby had a song for it.

To crown the magnificence, that lucky old sun came rolling up from distant seas to blind us all with his brilliance, turning night into the clarity of day, a brittle light which cast eerie shadows on the grey, delta wings of Concorde.

It might have been the space capsule on its way to the Moon, arousing the emotions of a journey to the land of our childhood dreams. You tried to grasp and absorb it but it slipped away from you as poignant moments do.

Then we banked to the right, turning our back on that paradise of northern light, and headed southwards to Scotland's dead of night.

There was time to catch up on the technicalities. From the aircraft's point of view, the engineers on board had been recording all kinds of information, from stress and strain at altitudes to the pattern of fuel consumption.

But the main purpose of the flight was to provide a vehicle for the scientists. Dr Harris and Mr Moss—boffins are better without first names!—were engaged in the interesting survey of the ozone layer in the upper atmosphere.

This is the protective gas which saves the earthly mortal from the damaging rays of the sun.

There is a theory that supersonic aircraft might adversely affect that protection and expose us to dangers. The theory may well turn out to have little substance but the scientists want to check the facts.

So they twiddled knobs and devoured statistics from dials and tapes which will presumably make sense to somebody back at the laboratory.

The non-scientific passenger resumed his seat and realised that, on the inside, Concorde is not noticeably different from any other modern plane.

At that height—and even at 1,360 miles an hour—there is little sensation of movement.

Concorde just seems to hang in space like a hovering vulture, perhaps waiting to snatch up an Orkney island for breakfast. There might be sonic bangs for the people down below, but up here there is nothing.

Just a smooth descent which takes us in over Fraserburgh, down to Aberdeen, and diagonally across Scotland to Prestwick.

The lady who served you at the tea-bar just three hours earlier is still there to serve you again.

When you tell her that you've been to the Arctic Circle, seen the sun rising and setting and that you will see a repeat performance on land before the day is over, her mouth falls open.

There is no doubt that the full magic of Concorde, due to fly commercially in 1975, will fire public imagination in supersonic fashion.

DAD'S DAY OF SPORTS GLORY
—THEN THE RAINS CAME

——————— *14th June 1973* ———————

There is, of course, something at least faintly ridiculous about those doting fathers to whom it is a matter of some moment that Little Baggypants does well at the school sports.

You know the sort. Tending towards flab, they didn't exactly make it in their own particular day but they're determined that Junior will.

So, having subjected the poor kid to the lies and boredom of an imagined glory, which eluded the Guinness Book of Records only by a printer's error, they call for an upholding of family tradition.

The caricature of such an ass was occupying my idle thoughts the other day as I wandered in the local park— the school field, as it happened—with my two younger sons.

If I was seen to assume a crouching position, it was really no more than an attempt to tie my shoelaces. That sudden sprint forward from the shoelaces was occasioned by a sudden twinge of lumbago, I swear.

But the boys found it amusing and we did it again and again, prefacing the lumbago jump, with a jocular cry of "Go!"

"See how fast you can run to that goalpost and back,"

I said in careless challenge. "I'll time you."

And there I stood, one eye on the youthful athletes and one on the seconds hand of my watch. Hmm. Fast boys these. Worth encouraging, eh? But come now! Mustn't behave like one of those silly fathers.

Now Sports Day was yesterday and, as fortune would plan it, that happened to be my day-off, which explains why I was heading briskly for the arena while most mothers were still applying the mascara and fathers were decently at work.

In time, the show was on. Class after class of infant prodigies came forward to the starting line before charging along an avenue of proud and prejudiced parents.

And there was nothing but admiration for this gaggle of geese—and every one of them a swan.

A fluttering in my breast, which might have been no more than a butterfly getting entangled in my semmit, seemed to stir as the young Websters came forward to the starting point.

The big moment was nigh. My self-control was admirable. Any second now and the pound of familiar feet could tell me what my heart wanted to know.

And then the unpredictable happened. With his strangely twisted sense of humour, the god of mockery intervened. Up sprang one of those rogue clouds which bedevil our Scottish climate and what he had to unload in the way of aquatic volumes was nobody's business.

Down it came in all its teeming tons, as teachers and children ran for shelter and spectators covered themselves in waterproofs and confusion.

I just stood there in defiance, the embodiment of anger and misery, raindrops gurgling in my earholes and drenching every part of my anatomy to the very seat of power.

Dreams went down drain-pipes and pride was swallowed up in puddles, leaving nothing but the solemn dignity of a drookit rat.

The sports resume tomorrow, they say. But I doubt if I'll be there. Not unless the editor insists that I take another day off. And then I might have to.

GEORGE MACKAY BROWN—
A PORTRAIT OF A NATURAL MAN

26th June 1973

There is no reply at the house looking down on the Stromness waterfront and the woman from the wee shop comes out to say: "George has gone for his messages, but hold on . . . here he comes along the street."

So I wait round the corner and prepare to take in my first sight of George Mackay Brown, one of the most highly-rated poets and short story writers of the day, who lives by the pen in his native Orkney, from which he seldom departs.

And there he is, a lean and rustic figure in big bonnet with the look of a shy boy—a young face, yet an old face, old as the hills and crags and battered shores of the land which fathered him.

He is, in fact, 51, a bachelor who views the world from the picturesque wynd of Stromness, where he grew up as youngest of five in the family of a local tailor-cum-postie.

His early manhood was dogged by tuberculosis, but long spells in a sanatorium gave him a chance to read and find inspiration in Yeats and T. S. Eliot and Gerard Manley Hopkins.

Later in life he took an honours degree in English at Edinburgh University, having already been a student at

Newbattle Abbey College when that other great Orkney poet, Edwin Muir, was Warden.

Soon he was returning to his native islands. In his middle age the ill-health has resolved itself into a chronic bronchitis but he works away steadily and has never been more productive than now.

"The wells of poetry have dried up somehow," he says over coffee. "But then you couldn't keep a cat on what you make out of poetry anyway.

"I have a novel about St Magnus, the patron saint of Orkney, coming out in September, followed by a book of short stories and a children's book, and I have finished a television play—and the Strathclyde Theatre Group are coming to Orkney this week to present two pieces of mine, *Witch* and *Return of the Women*."

Not that material gain ranks highly with George Mackay Brown. There were long, lean spells, he admits, when it was hard to survive. The Arts Council Literature Prize in 1969, for his collection of stories called *A Time to Keep*, was a help. "But, at present, I can exist on the sales of my work alone," he says. "Of course, it might be different if I had a wife and children to support, but I'm myself and it is a fairly simple life.

"I write between breakfast and lunch for five days a week, write letters on Saturday and maybe have a couple of pints on Sunday. In the afternoon I usually go shopping or meet friends.

"It's a good place for working up here. Plenty of peace and not many distractions."

George Mackay Brown radiates a simple courtesy. The face has flat cheek bones and jutting jaw, a crescent-moon which shines a kindly light.

Orkney is the haven where there is peace but, more, a sense of protection for those older standards he holds so dear.

The result is a natural man, patently genuine in his genius, writing what is honestly felt without thought of fashion or cult.

It may not, does not, always please the people of Orkney, whose island life is his immediate canvas.

Apart from the writers who inspired him, he says he also gained strength from his conversion to the Roman Catholic faith. His parents had been adherents to the Church of Scotland. He doesn't make a song about it but he goes to Mass when he can.

When you leave, he will take his farewell at the door and still be there waving gently from the window.

George Mackay Brown doesn't swamp you with words. But the quiet power of his sincerity (like the quiet power of his writing) washes over you and leaves a tide-mark that is hard to define.

And you walk away feeling refreshed and feeling better about people, and slightly haunted still by the experience.

OUR DAY FOR SOME
SUNRISE AND SHINE

———————— *9th July 1973* ————————

There had been this long-standing promise to my son that, one fine summer morning, I would get up with him in time to see the sunrise.

Like many other children of his age, he is fascinated by the universe and the spin of the earth and its distance from the sun.

So yesterday seemed as good a morning as any.

The alarm was set for 4.15am and Keith, who is eight and an early riser by nature, was quickly through to poke me awake. We dressed and were stepping up the street in 15 minutes.

It was a bright, clear sky on a still morning, with streaks of distant cloud already catching the early warnings of sunrise.

The horizon, looking north and eastwards over Glasgow's Linn Park, had that expectancy of a glorious Hollywood set.

At any moment, I thought, the strings of Carmen Dragon's orchestra would swell into a symphony which would surely bring people dancing from their doorways.

But the sounds were different. The residents lay quiet in their suburban boxes, calm except for the cry of a baby.

SUNRISE

The sounds came more from nature's early birds.

Crows cawed in the trees behind Williamwood golf course, with a muted counter-point from nearby owls, while smaller birds interrupted the breakfast feast of ground-level insects for a puzzled look at the morning strangers.

On the hillock of Beechgrove Park all was beautifully quiet as we talked about the speed and tilt of the earth and the 93 million miles to the sun.

The peace was disturbed only by an offending car racing down Clarkston Road, with that rasping exhaust which usually belongs to show-offs.

Late-night people, on their way home from a Saturday night party, we thought. Not real early-morning people like us. And we felt suitably superior.

Now there was the first sharp glint on the horizon. It was 5am, and within seconds, the sun was rising from its bed in the woods, big and red and bright, extending a warm welcome to the new day.

What a shame, we thought, there were not more people around to share and respond.

Surely this was the best of the light. Before long, the intrusion of cloud would likely mar this wonderland and turn it into another featureless day.

We went home glad we had risen for the sunrise.

Now it was 5.30 and time to go back to bed for a few hours' sleep.

The lady in the bed turned over, complaining of the disturbance, grunting about the fool I was.

And maybe she was right.

WHERE GOLF BALLS TAKE
OVER FROM JETS

12th July 1973

That they have diverted the planes (but not their noise) from their flight paths into Prestwick Airport this week is, in itself, a fair measure of the power and importance of the Open.

Golf balls instead of Boeings are taking off with the ultimate speeds of human propulsion and coming in to land at Troon with a direction which draws gasps from the countless thousands who are here for wonder and inspiration.

For the second year running, the greatest golfing competition in the world has come to Scotland—home because, lest we forget (and we never shall) it was Scotland which gave golf to the world.

And the world has not been slow to give it back, polished and perfected and packaged in stars and stripes or various other patterns—and played as those founding fathers of the Scottish fairways dreamed of.

We must go back to 1931 and Tommy Armour to find a Scottish winner. But we can keep on trying.

There were moments of hope and pride yesterday when David Webster of Lundin Links shot into the lead, only to be displaced by another homester in Harry Bannerman of

Banchory.

Could it be? Would it be?

The less romantic were looking for their winner among cool machines of golfing precision like Tom Weiskopf, Jack Nicklaus or the effervescent Lee Trevino.

All were agreed, however, on the sheer dramatic intensity of the occasion. From the clearing of early morning mists and the massive influx of cars from every direction, one could sense that this was going to be the greatest Open of them all.

There were four days of play ahead on this magnificent stretch of Ayrshire coast, with the waters of the Clyde on one side and a sea of marquees on the other, dispensing anything from pies and pints to fullscale meals.

Genteel diners at the Troon Marine looked out with a privileged view on the passing hordes, those marvelling masses hooked by golf's addiction and trotting in colourful columns along the fairways to pause in the reverent silence for green shots, to sigh sympathetically for putts missed and to burst into peals of uninhibited cheering for shots like Trevino's last one.

It came in from an awkward corner off the green and rolled into that little cup as if by manual control.

The jubilant Lee, resplendent in blue sweater and cap, bowed and capered and was driven off in a funny little buggy to the interview room to tell the Press about his round.

He was not too despondent with his 75 ("a 67 will wipe that out"), but he reckoned that if the wind did not change or die down, or do something, he didn't have a chance.

Lee has been playing so much golf since he arrived in Scotland that he showed a pair of rough-skinned hands and said: "Honest, man, you'd think I was a gravedigger not a golfer."

Meanwhile, the excitement outside was gathering. The

purists were waiting for Nicklaus, the Golden Bear, coming in with Bert Yancey, the early leader, and Britain's own Brian Barnes.

The Bear was gaily decked out in checked pants and a yellow sweater to match his straw-coloured hair.

Grandstands were filled with a brightly assorted cross-section of the world's sporting public—Scotsmen tending to look like Americans and tartan-clad Americans doing their best to look like Scotsmen.

Big names from other areas of entertainment, like racing driver Jackie Stewart, comedians Jimmy Tarbuck and Kenny Lynch and football's Don Revie, are here among the assorted masses.

On the course the biggest roar of all went up for 71-year-old Gene Sarazen when he holed in one at the notorious Postage Stamp. It was all happening at Troon.

Chi Chi Rodriguez from Puerto Rico took off his sweater and reviewed his earlier impressions that Scotland was a land of snow and ice floes.

On Saturday a record-breaking 100,000 people will have graced the 1973 Open in this magnificent setting at Troon. And they will go home vowing, with much justification, that it is the greatest show on earth.

PS: The Open was won that year by America's Tom Wieskopf.

NOW SHOWING . . .
THE LAST OF THE VIKING

———————————— *4th August 1973* ————————————

The Sleeping Beauty has been flickering heavy eyelids in Largs this week.

For today she and a number of other Disney characters will usher out the Viking, the last of the cinemas in the Ayrshire holiday town.

What was hailed as the super-cinema of 1938, the scented picture palace of Cagney, Cooper and Deanna Durbin, has fallen victim of the general decline in interest.

It suffers defeat in the way that Vikings have always suffered defeat in this particular town. For it was here, more than seven centuries ago, that these Northern warriors met their Waterloo at the Battle of Largs.

I sat in the vast auditorium of the cinema and tried to bring its lifetime into perspective. In those early days they were showing *Snow White and the Seven Dwarfs* first time round.

They showed it again last week. But now the paintwork of the place has faded, the upholstery has worn thin and the Viking of the golden era had taken on that big, empty look of times passed by.

If the people of Largs are caring at all about the death

of their cinema then they are not showing it at the box-office, for there were no more than 20 of us there.

At a time when the cinema has given way to bingo and booze, it is perhaps not surprising that the Viking will soon be converted into a bottle store for Mr Wham, the whisky man.

George Palmer, the owner, stood in front of his cinema with its Viking galley-prow in a pool of still water, and talked of the problems of running a big cinema in the seventies.

"I used to own three cinemas in Largs alone and there would be long queues," he told me. "But how can you keep going with 200 or 300 people in a hall which holds about 1,400?

"The situation has become hopeless. Until a few years ago the choice of film was mine, but now they are in short supply and that makes it even more difficult.

"The public just seems to want sex and violence," said George Palmer, who doesn't look the kind of man to give them either.

"Largs used to be a popular little place, with holiday makers coming from Glasgow and England to spend a fortnight. Nowadays they come for the day by car, have a fish supper, throw the paper in the gutter and go home."

He and his wife Janet are the only directors and, for Mrs Palmer, this week's closure is the heartbreak of losing her favourite cinema. She puts it down to bingo and coloured television.

But, if the Palmers are sorry to see it go, the Lappins are no less upset. For William Lappin, the manager, was projectionist there when the cinema opened.

It was launched by Lord Glasgow, he remembers, with a first offering of *Blondie*. And he remembers even more about the young usherette, Chrissie Withers, because he married her.

In the years between, the couple have been caught up in three other closures—at Partick, Giffnock and Scotstoun—but when her husband went back as manager five years ago, Mrs Lappin returned as cashier.

She talks nostalgically about those early red-and-white uniforms, for those were her years of romance. And now their connection with the cinema world is coming to a close.

The full-sized cinema has gone and, in the time-honoured way of the Vikings, they will push this particular monarch out to sea tonight. And he will burn away to quiet embers.

But just as the glow from those embers will surely die a new light will hopefully emerge.

George Palmer, who has never given up hope of salvaging something of the silver screen for Largs, has succeeded in acquiring a former restaurant near the sea front and plans to convert it into a small luxury cinema later this year.

THE MAN IN BLACK—WITH
A LITTLE TOUCH OF TARTAN

———————— 5th September 1973 ————————

With all the power and personality which elevated him to the throne of Country and Western music, Johnny Cash will launch the new Apollo Centre in Glasgow tonight to the acclaim of an adoring throng.

And for the Man in Black it will be much more than just another whistle-stop on a European tour.

For Johnny Cash, now 41, with the strong good looks of a modern Beethoven, is delighted to have uncovered the secret of his long-unexplained love of playing Glasgow.

When the thunderous applause of Manchester had subsided, he eased his massive frame into an inadequate hotel chair and told me:

"A relative of mine, Marie Cash, has given me the family tree and I have discovered that we are directly descended from a William Cash, who emigrated from Scotland—I believe from Glasgow—to Virginia in 1673.

"Now on this tour, of all the cities where we could have stayed for a second night, I have chosen Glasgow."

But what of this man whose hypnotic drawl would lull an audience to a trance if he were not at the same time stimulating them to a full awareness? What of the man who loves to play before an audience of convicts, who got caught in the trap of drug addiction and fought his way to freedom?

"I know our national leaders and politicians get involved in scandals and so on but I'm not at all pessimistic about the human race," he says.

"We are not going down the drain. Sure, there's a lot of inhumanity around but my daddy can tell you, from the time he was a boy there has always been trouble in the world. The preachers in 1900 were speaking about it. People have always been killing each other. It is just that there are more people around nowadays and more of it going on.

"The drug problem is not as bad as people think and I believe that alcoholism is still the biggest problem. There are, of course, some serious drug problems and my advice to the young is simply this: Don't try them. The trips are not worth it.

"Coming down is a whole lot harder than going up, as I can tell from personal experience. Fortunately I managed to overcome it but not many people can do so."

Johnny Cash has the air of a man who has grappled with a floodtide of inner forces, which could have gone either way, and has managed to channel them to good purpose. At the weekend he was appearing with Billy Graham at Wembley. Is there a growing religious side to his life?

"Yes, Christ is playing more and more part in my life. I think Christians should be affiliated to a church but that is of secondary importance to a connection with Christ. A man's best sermon is the life he leads.

"As for Billy Graham, I see him from time to time and he is such a powerful spiritual force that some of him is bound to rub off.

"You must believe in people. I am looking for less crime on our streets so I believe you must make better citizens of the men in prison to ensure that there won't be such a high percentage going back. The best way is to have a programme of teaching them to do something worthwhile in this world."

The man from Nashville, Tennessee, whose dark, square-cut looks confirm the proportion of Cherokee blood in his veins, prefers to put his views into song, which he does with legendary success, never failing to strike a chord of recognition in other people.

"I've been writing songs as long as I can remember and I guess I always shall, because I can say things there that I don't know any other way to say.

"I'm glad my business is booming. Country music has always been popular but nowadays there are more and more radio stations programming it and people all over the place are growing to love it."

Around him are artists like Carl Perkins, a pioneer of Rock 'n' Roll, and the famous Tennessee Three, all of whom Johnny Cash acclaims like brothers.

Appearing with Johnny in Glasgow will be his wife June Carter; he is also being accompanied on the tour by his father, 76-year-old Ray Cash.

Last time Johnny Cash was in Glasgow in 1971 his dressing-room was a tunnel under the stage, with a plastic washing-up bowl and soggy lump of soap. He'll find quite a change today. His dressing-room has colour telly, wall-to-wall carpets, dimming lights, walk-through shower unit, and even a bar.

REALLY STONED!
JUMPING JACK, JAGGER'S BACK

———————— *17th September 1973* ————————

Glasgow was really stoned last night—as the Stones rolled on in the Apollo Centre, trying to raise the roof.

The worshippers were there in time for a warm-up from Billy Preston, to drink Cola in the 30-minute interval and then to build up a chanting climax of anticipation for the king himself.

And there he was—30-year-old Mick Jagger, the man who took the trousers off sex in the sixties.

Bathed in a flood of red light, he came bouncing on stage to the rhythms of *Brown Sugar*, jumping, gyrating, waving, pouting, commanding and wearing his blue-sequinned trousers and familiar belt.

Lights lowered to a blue haze as he slid his way into the current hit of *Angie* but that was mere contrast for the next burst of energetic gymnastics.

Sometimes he would just stand up for admiration, a rare combination of Beauty and the Beast, having dried himself of the pouring sweat.

As he stirred them up with *Tumbling Dice* and *Honky Tonk Woman*, the audience were on their feet, pleading for anything which Jagger was prepared to give.

273

They answered his clapping commands like puppets on a string, dazed by the spell of their idol.

Bouncers kept a check on excessive displays of exhibitionism in the audience but, in the truth, how can you put on a show like this, with an appeal which is mostly below the belt, and expect to contain the ensuing frenzy? It's unreasonable.

So the whole show blazed and blared to a white-hot climax with rainbow lighting and smoke bombs and Jagger pouring a ladle of water over his own head and then splashing one over his audience.

A final crescendo . . . and darkness . . . and they were gone . . . and the crowd were screaming for more.

As an actor and showman, Jagger is truly magnificent. But magnificent or not, he was not having an encore. He had in fact already left the building said an announcer.

Just to calm the place, they played a canned version of *Land of Hope and Glory*, followed by *Greensleeves*. You might have thought we had never departed from dear old grandma's day.

STILL MARCHING ON—
AT NINETY YEARS OLD

————————— *4th October 1973* —————————

In the late years of life, G. Stanley Smith looks out upon a peaceful autumn setting of lawns and bushes and pleasant Surrey countryside and remembers springtime in Hillhead, Glasgow. It was there he was born, in 1888, into the home of that famous Scotsman, William Alexander Smith, founder of the Boys' Brigade.

That laudable organisation, which began humbly enough in a mission hall in North Woodside Road, grew to encircle the world and to set a pattern for youth organisation which was widely followed.

William Smith harnessed the energies of boyhood and found widespread support from men like Major-General Baden-Powell, who later extended the good work by forming the Boy Scouts.

Today, the Boys' Brigade has a world membership of more than 265,000 including 54,000 in Scotland. And today they will remember their founder on this, the 90th anniversary of his very first company, the 1st Glasgow.

Torch-bearers will carry messages from that original mission hall to B.B. headquarters in Bath Street, then on to George Square and finally to Glasgow Green.

About 1,200 boys will parade for a festival of music and fireworks and to hear a message from the Queen.

There will be a message, too, from Stanley Smith, a witness of the past, from that nursing home near Haslemere. He followed his father as full-time secretary of the Boys' Brigade.

"My whole life has been centred on the Brigade," he told me. "From those childhood days when our home was at 12 Hillsborough Terrace. I remember it as a happy home, a place where groups of boys would gather for evenings.

"My father had come down from Thurso, when his father died, to work in his uncle's office in Princes Square, just off Buchanan Street, Glasgow. Then he went into the shipping business himself.

"Meanwhile, he had become an officer in the 1st Lanarkshire Volunteers and a teacher in the Mission Sunday School in North Woodside Road."

William Smith was puzzled that it was so easy to control 100 men in the Volunteers on Saturday and so difficult for some people to control a handful of boys on Sunday.

The answer, he reckoned, was to instil a sense of discipline and esprit de corps, to teach them elementary drill and physical exercise, obedience to the word of command, punctuality, and cleanliness.

He put his idea to two friends in a room in Woodside Quadrant, and the three knelt down and committed the future of the scheme to God. In that Glasgow mission hall, on October 4, 1883, the Boys' Brigade was born.

Within 10 years it had swept the world, with 300 companies in the United States and more than 70 in Canada. The diffident lad from Thurso, still in his thirties, was acclaimed at rallies in far corners of the earth.

With the motto, "Sure and Stedfast," he taught the world to value the qualities of boyhood, to which he had added a sense of purpose and an even greater idealism.

THE WELCOME RETURN OF
NEIL PATERSON—NOVELIST

—————————— *24th October 1973* ——————— ———

In the early days of his career he was hailed as Scotland's greatest storywriter since Robert Louis Stevenson.

But since 1953 there has not been a single book from the pen of Neil Paterson, son of a Banff solicitor, master of the short story, who acquired an army of followers with *The China Run* and *Behold Thy Daughter*.

So I was delighted, when I unearthed him this week, to find that he was putting the final touches to a novel, set in Italy, with the provisional title, *A Candle for the Devil*.

What about those missing 20 years? They have not been idle or unprofitable. Neil Paterson has quietly become one of the world's most successful film writers, wooed by every major company.

He has spent about three months in every 12 in California, become the acquaintance of stars like Cary Grant and Stewart Grainger and won an Oscar for the film script of *Room at the Top*.

Through it all, he has resolutely refused overtures to work in Hollywood.

He reckons the sensible place to write, even for the hurly-burly of the movie world, is the sleepy little Perthshire town of Crieff, where I found him at work.

Neil Paterson's athletic build and youthful turn belie his 57 years (as a youth he was a fine footballer, captaining Dundee United at the age of 20). The green, wide-set eyes are alert as ever. The hair has turned to a distinguished grey-white since last I saw him but otherwise there is little change. Had he no regrets about forfeiting a place among the immortal writers for the greater rewards of Hollywood?

"I never saw it like that," he began. "I have no great message to give, no windmills to tilt at which are not being titled at all the time. I was not seduced by Hollywood, it is just that I am a story-writer; dialogue has always been the strength of whatever talent I may possess and I have simply been telling stories on film.

"Of course, it is true that I am a professional writer and novels tend to be poor reward for your efforts. You can make 50 times more from a film.

"It all began when I wrote *The Kidnappers*, starring Duncan Macrae and the two Aberdeenshire schoolboys. I found I could do this. Then I went on to films like *High Tide at Noon*, *The Shiralee*, *Innocent Sinner* and *Room at the Top*.

"I wrote the story of *Man on the Tightrope*, but I didn't do the film script.

"It is the way of things in the film world that you write considerably more than ever sees the light of day. For a variety of reasons, including lack of financial backing, many productions just don't happen.

"I was engaged on *Forty Days of Musa Dagh*, which was to have been one of those four-hour films. But it never reached the screen."

To raise money for films, the Hollywood moguls are inclined to tell one party that another is willing to put up so much money. Then they tell the other party the same story—in the hope that both will come up with the cash. Likewise, they bargain with talent.

"They tried to interest me in a film to be called *The Stepmother*," says Paterson. "I wasn't too interested, though I saw some possibilities in it, but I was told that Ingrid Bergman was absolutely crazy about doing this film.

"So I saw her in Paris and we had lunch and discussed it and I said: 'Tell me, why are you so crazy to do this one?' She replied: 'I'm not crazy about it. But they told me YOU were!' It never did become a film."

His involvement in the strangely anonymous world of big-time script-writing has not diverted his attention from the cultural life of his native land. Indeed, Neil Paterson has probably done more for promoting the arts in Scotland these past 12 years than any other person.

As well as his work for the Arts Council, he is production chairman for Films of Scotland, that Government-establishment body which turns out up to 10 films a year. He is a director of Grampian Television.

Neil Paterson, who began his career with a prolific output for the cheap magazines, sits down at his desk every morning. Whether he writes or not is another matter.

He may just relax to chat about his wife and grown-up family of three, or his grandfather, the famous Mr Kerr who gave us Kerr's Pink potatoes; or enthuse about Scotland's chances in the World Cup.

Even before the movie world put his economic mind at ease, Neil Paterson was a man of style and easy manner. As he puts the final touches to his new book, he will tell you that it is all about a bastard.

More legitimately, it is not without its possibilities as a film.

GETTING A SALUTE FROM
MY MIDDLE-AGED HEROES

The vibration of the Second World War had affected us little in our sleepy backwater village of Maud, in Aberdeenshire.

But an excitement was gathering that day in October, 1942, when word spread round the school playground that soldiers were coming to billet themselves in our midst.

And soon they were rolling in, men of the 4th Battalion, The King's Own Scottish Borderers, with their Bren-gun carriers and trucks and pipe band and military band, in numbers which trebled our modest population.

As they took over the village hotel and hall and the nearby Brucklay Castle, we ran down after school to savour the excitement.

I latched on to the pipe band, and particularly to Pipe Sergeant Jock Gray, who agreed to teach me to play in return for running the band's messages.

Our whole parish opened its hearts to these mill workers and farm servants and tradesmen from Hawick and Jedburgh, Galashiels, Melrose and Kelso, whom we came to regard as the salt of the earth.

Then on May Day, 1943, the soldiers lined up, shook hands with the village folk and marched away to their next camp in Aberdeen.

I marched with them. They fell out for a rest at Auchnagatt and when they re-formed Captain Frank Coutts, the Scottish International Rugby player, came back and said: "I think you should be running home now, son. Your mother will wonder where you are." I was broken-hearted.

Well, except for the few who came back on visits I never saw any of them again. Not, that is, until Saturday night when I drove south on a very special journey to Hawick.

It was the 27th annual reunion dinner, and there was the kid from Maud, an honoured guest at the top table, looking down rows of faces which I had known in the freshness of their twenties and thirties, now mellowed to the lines of fifties and sixties.

Speaking has long been one of my defects but the chairman asked me to say a few words. So I got up and said they might like to know how they had seemed, 30 years ago, through the eyes of an 11-year-old boy.

When I finished my impromptu tribute to these men of the Blue Bonnets, they rose to their feet, with customary unison, and gave me what is commonly known as a standing ovation.

It rang loud and long and sincere and it gave me one of the richest moments of my life.

GRAND OLD LADY
STILL HAS STYLE

Once upon a time there was a lady called St Enoch, who became the mother of St Mungo, who became the patron saint of Glasgow.

And in 1879 her name was used for a new railway hotel being built by the old Glasgow and South Western.

In no time at all, it had blossomed into the most sophisticated place in town, attracting a clientele which ranged down the years from King Edward VII, in his days as the Prince of Wales, to Noel Coward and Ida Lupino.

The St Enoch was one of Europe's top hotels, as well as the very first public building in Scotland to be lit by electricity.

But, in the cause of what is commonly called progress, the surgery of Dr Beeching removed the adjoining station, which had been the original focal point, and made way for a giant car park.

Now the planners talk of redevelopment and the whole place will be pulled down to make way for a modern complex, which will include a new hotel.

Until that day comes, the Grand Old Lady of central Glasgow lives out her days in a dignity which you don't find in your glass-and-chrome palaces.

But she plans a belated flirtation. She is making a bid to woo the average car-park customer who tucks his saloon into the former railway station and passes the imposing doorway on his way to the nearest snack-bar.

So you can safely mount those stately steps, sample the spacious grandeur of a departed age—and dine adequately for less than £1.

To mark the transformation, Mr Douglas McDermid, the hotel manager, has taken the starch out of the main dining-room, given it the challenging name of the Claymore Restaurant and introduced such recognisable dishes to the à la carte menu as haggis and ham-and-haddie, both priced at 50p.

There is pâté St Enoch at 30p and nothing more damaging to the pocket than a grilled fillet steak (six ounces) with mushrooms and tomato for £1.30.

Such an economic arrangement in surroundings of four-star grace and comfort is not an every-day encounter, but I sampled it yesterday. And will be doing so again . . . while the going's good.

COME FLY WITH ME . . .
AND MEET THE FAR EAST
SCOTS CONNECTION

——————— *24th December 1973* ———————

DATELINE: HONG KONG

Along the Chater Road of Hong Kong the lights were twinkling brightly with messages of seasonal greeting.

Loudspeakers blared out a version of *I'm Dreaming of a White Christmas* which, in Hong Kong's climate, must surely be a dream indeed.

The fashionable Mandarin Hotel proudly announced its Christmas cabaret act—"the pure, lyrical voice of Scotland's Moira Anderson."

And all around was the clang and clutter of downtown Hong Kong, tramcars from a bygone day bursting with Chinese faces, wizened women with children on their backs, faces resigned to sadness but graceful still.

Already the energy shortage has meant a 10.30 curfew on all neon signs, a restriction which has brought warning from club owners that government buildings will be subjected to a protest march—from their topless barmaids. Yes, Hong Kong is full of eastern promise.

Lights or no lights, the very name rings out with a magic which stirs up all sorts of exotic pictures.

You sense its excitement from the moment the plane

comes precariously over Kowloon, a mainland section of the colony, trimming slummy skyscrapers from which bamboo poles project with washing like the bunting for a coronation.

The plane comes in to land at Kai Tak, in the most extra-ordinary setting of an airport anywhere, close by the bustling traffic of the most concentrated community in the world.

You are in no doubt that you have reached Hong Kong, capitalist colony which clings to Communist China like a fly to a bull.

There are five million people living in Hong Kong, as if you had taken all Scotland and crammed it on to Arran.

Indeed, it seems at times as if someone *had* taken all Scotland and done just that.

For Scots are everywhere. Across in the heart of Kowloon, which you reach by the chug of the Star Ferry from the island, the 1st Battalion of the Black Watch are entrenched in the heart of a bustling community.

The accent rings out, too, among sailors and airmen, policemen, business men and footballers. There's a story to them all.

I met a chap with the Chinese name of Ling Kei-lee, who used to be better known to me as former Glasgow colleague Drew Rennie. He recently became public relations boss of the Hong Kong police, a testing task if ever there was one, in view of the corruption uncovered within that force.

Upstairs in the police bar, I bumped into the deputy boss of the anti-corruption squad, big Alistair McNutt, whose father was minister at Udny Green, Aberdeenshire, and who was to discover that corruption investigation, like charity, was to begin at home.

As darkness falls, you find your way into the downtown bars and clubs of Kowloon and Wanchai, which offer their distinctive attractions. A grubby staircase gives little hint of the plush surroundings in Club-the-World, where soft lights and music and not-so-soft drink and women intermingle in a heady brew.

Suddenly, you realise that you are very much in the world of Suzie Wong, among the taxi-girls who are there for the buying-out at negotiable rates.

Out into the night and the permitted lighting of Hong Kong twinkles up through Mid Levels to the Peak, which dominates all else.

Beyond the mountains lies Communist China, a world away.

Thereabouts, I would say,
the Swinging Sixties petered out. . . .